TODAY'S SOUND

A *Melody Maker* book

edited by
Ray Coleman

Hamlyn

London   New York   Sydney   Toronto

Originally published in the United Kingdom
as 'The Melody Maker File'
by IPC Specialist and Professional Press Limited

This edition published by the
Hamlyn Publishing Group Limited
London   New York   Sydney   Toronto
Astronaut House, Feltham, Middlesex, England

© Copyright IPC Specialist and Professional Press Limited 1973

Reprinted 1974

ISBN 0 600 36142 X

Printed in England by
Chapel River Press Limited, Andover, Hampshire

The Year of Outrage

Alice Cooper

by Michael Watts

Shep Gordon is here, there and everywhere, racing across the stage of this small, red-plush theatre or pacing up and down the centre aisle between the rows of empty seats; he is waving his arms and calling out directions, a clipboard in one hand, like everyone's idea of how a stage producer should act.

It would be just perfect if he flung out those arms and said, "no luv, you make your entrance from the left," but he's not Peter Brook and this isn't, strictly speaking, a theatre production.

Shep Gordon is just the other side of the tracks, in the rock and roll pasture, where there's more money in being illegit.

Despite his somewhat untypical rimmed glasses and slightly balding, fuzzy head, which make him appear collegiate, he is, at age 26, the hottest manager in the rock business.

And up there, centre stage, with the can of Budweiser in his hand, is the reason: Alice Cooper, pop's very own grisly bare figure.

Cooper and Gordon. The two of them have created a rock and roll penny dreadful, a slice of punk melodrama, which this year sprang evermore luridly to life on a 56-city tour of north America that on paper looked certain to gross more than the Stones' tour of the States in 1972.

1973 would seem to be the year in which all segments of the public have to come to some terms with this 20th century Gothic phenomenon.

Strategically, Alice Cooper has become so successful over an accelerating period of two years through a highly astute assessment of the spirit of the times and a shrewd application of gimmicks to that end. We are living in an era where the

5

nerve ends of mass consciousness appear to be deadened; where the taste buds need to be further and further stimulated by the injection of one outrage or another; where the second most commercially successful movie in the whole of America is the porno flick, Deep Throat, in which one penis after another is seen tickling a pair of female tonsils. The morality of it is incidental.

The facts are that it's hard to be surprised, let alone shocked, by anything that happens anymore.

In this context Alice Cooper is a titillation, a sour chuckle. He is also an exploitation: in this case of the atmosphere of sex and violence which lives tangibly on the streets of America and on its television and cinema screens.

It's no coincidence that of the two main practitioners of theatrical rock, as its become tritely known, Cooper should be American and Bowie British.

The latter upholds a serious, traditionally "artistic" aesthetic, and plays it all for real, whereas Cooper assumes the sleazy glamour and generally ersatz quality of the Hollywood B-movie; he's much more a descendant of pop culture and all its throwaway aspects than is Bowie.

He exploits, furthermore, in the grand old manner of pop: he gives the public exactly what it wants and takes it a little bit further each time so as to hone the edge of that expectation.

Just like the Who, who exploited their generation of the mods.

Whether you like Alice Cooper or not probably depends on whether you're of that generation in their late teens. If not, acceptance hinges on a sense of humour.

There's no other way to take a song like "I Love The Dead," say, on Alice's album, "Billion Dollar Babies." The theme is necrophilia, and it's as cheap and nasty as it sounds, with lines like "while friends and lovers mourn your silly grave, I have other uses for you, darling."

I can envisage the pseudo-

6

intellectuals among us conducting a brief for this as a kind of litany of shock therapy, permissible because it breaks into a previously forbidden area for music.

On the other hand, the professors of punk music will love it because of its supreme tastelessness.

I've already read one reviewer who used the substance of this track in calling Alice Cooper "the real pervert genius of the 70s." This is the sort of infantile criticism that believes if something is really bad it's glorious.

In fact, it is very funny in a sick-humour way, but it's more consistent with a Barry Humphries than a Lenny Bruce, who was much more than just a poseur with a sense of humour.

Alice has nothing to say, really, beyond what a lark it would be to screw some dead meat. Only the highly impressionable would describe this as genius.

There's no question, though, that that black humour in the Alice Cooper act has been increasingly defined.

It's readily apparent in their touring show, whose rehearsal I witnessed in Porchester, Connecticut, just before they took it to Canada for four, small experimental dates.

The first half of the show is pretty much straightforwardly musical with a run through of their singles hits and cuts from the new album; the exception is on "Unfinished Sweet," again from "Billion Dollar Babies," which is an ode to tooth decay and features some theatrics with a giant, mock drill and a man dressed inside a nasty-looking molar. It's harmless enough.

Then there is a taped intermission of "Night On Bald Mountain," a stentorian piece of music if there was ever one, during which roadies are seen dashing around the stage in the gloom spraying around dummy limbs and torsos (though I'm sure the uninitiated won't be aware of this).

When the band comes back Alice himself is dressed in black drapes, as opposed to the white duds of the first half, so you're well aware that this is where the action begins.

They cut into "Sick Things" and "Dead Babies," where Alice hunches himself over the splayed-out legs of a dummy model of a woman. He then jabs a sword he's carrying through the head of a doll and waves it around on the point.

So far the pattern of his act has been familiar. It's not totally unexpected, therefore, that the piece de resistance of it all should be a death scene, an execution.

The peculiarity of Alice Cooper shows is that they all involve retribution for the sins committed as a kind of pop "Crime and Punishment"; they invoke, consciously or not, a Hollywood code of good and bad. It may go down, in fact, that Cooper will be remembered for giving death popular appeal.

This time the chosen weapon of execution is not the gallows but the guillotine, and the grim humour of it is quite impressive.

He and Gordon have hired a magician, James Randy, who works under the name of the Amazing Randy. His speciality is a trick guillotine, and because magicians operate closed enclaves when you buy a trick you pay, too, for the guy who invented it.

Cooper, apparently, has long been interested in magic—on stage he himself flicks a flimsy handkerchief into a cane—and Randy is along for the act and also to entertain on the road.

For the guillotine scene Randy wears an executioner's hood of fur around his head and shoulders and Alice is dragged to La Guillotine wailing "I Love The Dead" while he postures like Richard the Third.

The stage twilight deepens except for a circle of light on his head, which is fastened between the two planks of wood.

Randy pulls on the piece of rope—even at the rehearsal everyone was breathlessly quiet—and the broad cleaver head, made of thick, heavy metal, falls swiftly.

All in an instant the light appears to shut off and then on again, and instead of Alice's tangled head of hair there's only a round, black hole.

Then, as "I Love The Dead" creaks once more with passable eeriness, the executioner dips into his basket set before the guillotine and pulls forth a rubber facsimile which even at close quarters bears a very good likeness to the original.

There are trickles and smears of blood from the lips. He carries this out to centre stage and then tosses it to the rest of the band, who pat it around among themselves like gleeful, malicious urchins.

It resembles nothing so much as the final scene in "Suddenly Last Summer": an act of lip-smacking cannibalism.

This is essentially the climax, although Alice comes back to unfurl the American flag and they all troop offstage to the strains of Kay Smith singing "God Bless America," returning just to deliver mock-military salutes to the audience.

One way or another, they go out of their way to offend fuddy-duddies. But then, there aren't likely to be many in their audiences.

The preparation for this show has gone on in earnest since Christmas, when designer Joe Gannon, who staged Neil Diamond at the Greek Theatre in Hollywood and the Winter Garden on Broadway, together with Tiny Tim at Caesar's Palace, was brought in.

He's put together a stage thirty feet deep and forty feet wide which is framed in winking, coloured lights, like a Tom Jones special.

The cost of this is around 150,000–175,000 dollars, but the overall production cost is up to 250,000 dollars.

Expenses of the whole tour, in fact, which necessitates taking 36 people on the road (including the support band, Flo and Eddie, and their people) are at a minimum of one million, two hundred thousand dollars.

But then they expect to gross at least 4.6 million, and that can go much higher—there are four extra dates in reserve for LA, two in Detroit and one in Philly.

Gannon — a thickset character

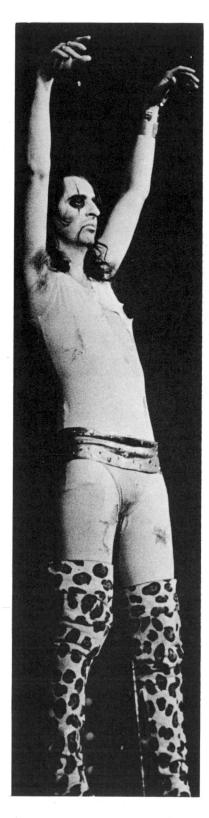

whose looks and personality are remarkably like Maynard Ferguson's —is particularly pleased to be on the road with Alice.

He signed the band to Zappa's and Herbie Cohen's Straight lable five years ago, when he was their A and R man. And he's known Shep Gordon, apparently, for longer than that. Before the Zappa deal he was proud manager with the Kingston Trio.

The press coverage is going to be intense. A chartered plane is taking press and groups down to Philadelphia tomorrow, and in all 56 cities of the tour there will be press conferences and lunches.

In cities on the later dates there will be displayed a hologram of Alice —a three-dimensional photograph made with refracted laser light—for which Cooper's Alive Enterprises has paid Salvador Dali 14,000 dollars.

Cooper, an impassioned Dali fan like the rest of the band, sat for the old monstre sacre one Sunday. They met almost a month earlier at the St Regis hotel in New York.

Alice had his usual six-pack of Bud and Dali asked for a glass of hot water into which he poured some honey—after snipping it off with a pair of scissors.

The hologram is a model of Cooper's brain with a chocolate eclair, representing his music, oozing out of it, and a number of other features, including a white fractured sculpture, symbolic of a microphone, and a soft watch—a rather tired surrealistic image one might feel.

For the occasion Alice wore a million dollars' worth of diamonds around his chest and hair that once belonged to the Duke of Westminster, and six gunmen were there to ensure they weren't nicked. No details are being left to chance.

It was the day after the sitting saw the preview in Porchester, a small town about an hour's drive from New York and ten minutes from the Alice Cooper estate in Greenwich, Connecticut. Dummy legs and arms were lying around the seats in the first few rows of the theatre.

The band had got a new snake that day, as yet unnamed, and it was coiled in its small, glass vivarium. The cans of Bud were littered like ciggie butts.

There seemed a few real problems with the rehearsal. Bob Dolan has been added on keyboards and Mick Mashbir on supplementary guitar to help out Glen Buxton, the lead, who's recuperating from pancreatis but was playing vigorously and none the worse for wear.

And Shep Gordon was in turn animated and thoughtful. He and Alice did all the conferring.

At one point Ashley Pandel, Alice's head of promotion, said he was glad to God he wasn't Shep Gordon. If you only knew the problems . . . why, in two years he'd watched him lose some hair. And he, Shep, had turned down offers from BIG groups, just to concentrate his interest. And now Alice was considering offers for movies.

Ashley himself looked more dead than alive.

Driving home to New York, Alice sat in the back seat, the inevitable can of Budweiser in his paw. It should have been beer, not a microphone sculpture, for old Salvador.

He's genial, a good storyteller, and very funny. He flips on the car radio and it's some schmucky ballad about lost love. Softly but impishly he starts improvising between the lines. "She di-ed . . he drowned her . . . they found her floating in the bathtub . . ." He giggles and we all join in.

Driving back through Harlem he says would we mind stopping. He'd like to ask a Negro for his autograph. The Chambers Brothers told him that one.

Oh yes, Alice Cooper has a sense of humour, all right.

The Year of Outrage

David Bowie

by Roy Hollingworth

Charing Cross Station, London, 9.10 p.m.: And when he arrived they screamed and they cried, and they rushed, and gushed forth and beat their feverish feminine fists into the backs of the brave coppers who shielded HIM. For it is indeed HIM.

One girl, her face bloated, and most ugly with tears and ruddy emotion, fell half-way twixt train and rail. A young copper dragged her to safety. Ten yards down the platform HE was pretty close to injury too.

Bowie, despite all the fierce body-guarding, was being kissed, and pinched, and touched, and ripped at. His hair now untidy; his eyes wild; his mouth open. A picture of terror. But his open mouth also bore the shadow of a crazed smile. They pushed him against a carriage door.

It took burly constabulary to lift this small squirrel-haired figure to safety; his face now very creased with every emotion a face could ever squeeze itself into. And they squeezed him into a car that was battered, and clawed at. And that car squeezed

its way to safety. And Mr Bowie was back in England.

And on Platform One, in a dirty wet huddle, lay two plumpish girlies, crying, and holding each other, and just crying. Everyone had gone, except they. Their tights all ripped, their knickers showing. And they just lay there . . . crying.

That, my friends, is actually the end of the story. This arrival; this sweaty, shocking, swift and severe welcome home for Bowie, back from Japan, 7,000 miles by boat and train, because . . . because he won't fly.

Via Trans-Siberian Express, he "Bowied" Moscow, travelling "soft" in first class. Second class is called "hard." "And is indeed hard" said Bowie.

Four and a half months away from England. He travelled the world, and, unlike the rest, saw its people. No in and out of a hotel, and onto plane. He saw the people, And now Mr Bowie is a very changed man. And people are going to kill him with his concern for them. No

amateur dramatics. Mr Bowie is concerned.

So where does the story begin?

It begins in Terminal One lounge Heathrow Airport, waiting, seeing heavy rain spatter the runway / delay on flight / bad weather / We have to find Bowie in Paris / had to be found / BEA departure to Paris / "Will passengers avoid treading heavily on the gangplank as it is waterlogged" / Captain Black in charge / thunderstorm over Paris / Trident One hit by lightning three times / lands on a runway fit for a trawler.

Now you see why Bowie won't fly?

So where do we find him?

We find him at The George V Hotel—we don't see him, but we find him. A porter—out for a swift five francs—shows us to the Rouge Room where a Bowie reception was held. It was held. He lights a match: "Monsieur Bowie ees not 'ere." Nobody was there. The room was as black as a Guinness. We phone around.

I find—on the phone—Leee Black Childers. Now Leee was the MM's photographer in New York, but when Bowie appeared in New York, he became Bowie's photographer. I was annoyed—but not deeply.

"Yeah, David's here / Russia, wow / they loved him / gee they tried to take away my cameras / we've had such fun / why don't you see Cherry Vanilla?"

Now the last time I saw Cherry Vanilla was in a hotel room in New York where she preyed over a table like a vulture preys over the bones of fat explorers.

An ex-film starlet and groupie with much body and much voice. Now Bowie's "press aid." She ordered a table of things for me. Mostly wine. Which was never drunk. At £7 a bottle that might annoy people.

"Bowie was arriving in New York, and I was a groupie. And I knew the press. Christ I was a groupie" (she split her nightdress to reveal nothing underneath). "And there I was, and Mr Bowie gave me a job."

What job did he give you dear?

"His Press Lady."

How is he?

"Gee darling, I wish I knew."

I now know that it is in fact true that one can live in splendour doing not the slightest damned thing. Cherry Vanilla-ed on. And I left, and went to bed. £30 per night for a single room.

The very next morning Bowie was supposed to catch the 12.30 Paris-Victoria train. There's not even a twinkle from his room. Breakfast, £3, and then a cab to Paris Nord Station.

We don't know whether the lad is on the train or not. He hadn't left the hotel. I run the length of the train—22 coaches in search of the squirrel—haired kid. Twenty-two coaches, and he wasn't on it.

Mission impossible.

So Barrie Wentzell and I wait, somewhat dazed, awfully broke, and listening to the chatter on the intercom. It's no different from Charing Cross my dears except that they announce trains for Lyons instead of Tunbridge Wells. And the porters smoke Gitanes in preference to No. 6.

And then, as the sunlight split the smoke of several hundred smoking porters, there appeared in all innocence, and in neat suit of silver and purples, David Bowie. Fresh from a limousine, and with that delightful wife of his, Angie. "The most remarkable woman on Earth," says David. She might well be.

"So we've missed the bleedin' train," says David looking at Platform 4, all empty and trainless.

"Never mind dear," says Angie. "There's another soon," and she wiggles her American bottom, and vanishes to the inquiry desk.

"Seven thousand miles," says David, smiling, and very, very fresh, "and we miss the bleedin' train on the last leg. From Japan to Paris and we miss the train."

Well, we couldn't catch the next one for that involved a flight to Gatwick. And the next one involved taking a hovercraft from Boulogne to Dover. "Can't do it," says Bowie. "If it flies, it's death."

But David, it only flies a few inches above sea level.

"Then, for the first time in two years I shall leave the land," says Bowie.

Later, we board the train, and he's talking away. About music?

No my people. About the fate of the world.

He talked about the fate of the world for approximately two hours. Well, not just he, but we. "I have feelings that I know just what is going on. I have feelings."

The train rattles through Monsieur, or somewhere like that. "I might put them into songs. You know, these feelings."

Bowie still chain-smokes (almost everybody else's ciggies, not his own). Leee Childers lives behind his reflect-ing sun-shades. Cherry Vanilla vanillas on. Angie Bowie smiles, and is indeed very lovely.

"You see Roy," said Bowie, softly, looking straight at me, dead-eyed, a can of beer acting as the microphone, "I've gone through a lot of changes... A whole lot of changes. It's all happened on my way back from Japan. You see... I've seen life, and I think I know who's controlling this damned world.

"And after what I've seen of the state of this world. I've never been so damned scared in my life."

Are you going to write about it?

"If I did it would be my last album ever."

You mean that?

"It would have to be my last album ever."

Why?

"Because I don't think I'd be around after recording it."

Are you ill?

"I believe I am. I have a very strange pain in my right hand side. I've had it for a year. It's a pain that now has to be taken to a specialist."

His eyes are full of menace now—mainly because his belly's full of beer, which we all constantly drink. We pass a field of French beef, and Bowie starts to cough, and cough, and he can't stop. "The cough darling?" inquires Angie. Bowie answered her with this deep, frightening cough which for God's sake, starts somewhere in his stomach!

"The (cough) changes I've seen... they have to be written about."

Then YOU write them David! (I say).

"Yes (cough), I suppose somebody must (cough). I feel the weight of the world on my shoulders."

Yes, he could actually carry the world on his shoulders. It's all down to the cut of the jacket. The shoulders are very big.

My memory goes back to the platform on Paris Nord. They're piping out the music to "Last Tango in Paris." We were walking along, together, and talking about Lou Reed. "He's so damned fine," says Bowie.

"And they throw up all this mystery around him, and all this bloody silliness. Can't they understand that he's just a New York cat, and that is JUST what he is. You know it would be so nice if people would be able to see that beneath it all—we're all very easy people."

They'd never believe it David. They wouldn't want to.

"Maybe you're right. But we are easy people. And maybe in a lot of ways . . . very simple. If only they could see. Oh God this intellectual confusion that surrounds us all. Why . . . why . . . why?"

He carried his suitcase. "I know I'm sick of being Gulliver. You know, after America, Moscow, Siberia, Japan. I just want to bloody well go home to Beckenham, and watch the telly."

But back to the train. The talk of the state of the world continued, and became intense, and deep. We pooled our experiences. Shared thoughts, ideas.

"You know," said David. "The rock revolution did happen. It really did. Trouble was nobody realised when it happened. We have to realise now. Let me tell you, the 'underground' is alive and well—more alive than it has ever been."

The Train rasped, and clanked to a halt at Boulogne. Leee Childers and most of the party thought it was Calais—but it didn't really matter.

"Oh, the seaside, how very lovely. How nice," said Bowie kicking his shoes into the sand that surrounds the Hover-Port.

But then fear struck his face as he saw his next line of transport arrive.

The Channel was clear, and like (as they say) a millpond. The sun was strong, and clean, and then this thing roared into sight. It was like a sperm whale with propellers. And was very noisy . . . And most monstrous. "Oh, no," said David.

"Oh yes," said Angie. "They don't hurt David."

"But they fly."

Only inches above the sea David.

He sat, and hardly said a word during the "flight." He was worried. But it was safe. At the Hover-Port he'd met a couple of girlies. Sweet little things on a day trip to France. And they'd seen Bowie. And he talked to them, and signed their fag packets. They pinched themselves to see if it was real.

Dover. The white-cliffs, now actually amber as the sun sets. His feet on English soil. A waiting room on Dover Station. He had a cup of tea, and B.R. sausage roll. And then he talked, so nicely to girls on the platform.

"Roy, they're the salt of the earth. Those girls. They don't sit each night and compare notes of groups, criticising lyrics, asking if it's valid. They just play the record . . . yeh, and maybe they dance. I love them. I love them dearly."

More beer cans emerge as the train (a slow one) leaves Dover.

Miss Vanilla is asleep. So is Mrs

Bowie. David reads a London Evening Standard—and gets back into Brit-things (British Things). He laughs, and laughs. What a funny little country we are.

"I've got to work harder this year than I've ever worked in my life. You know that?" he'd said earlier twixt train and hovercraft. "We're going to do a 79 date tour of America this year in about as many days. I might die. But I have to do it."

"I mean, you know the Spiders have only played about 50 dates altogether. About time we started working I feel."

Through lavish English countryside the train trundled on. David and myself retire to a less crowded

David Bowie and wife Angie

compartment. In fact . . . we're on our own. Alone, together.

Are you aware of what you're going back to on this train David?

"Er, not really. No. Four and a half months away has put me out of touch with what you might call the English rock scene.

"I know that every little bag that we've been in up to now has been incredibly exciting. But now . . . well, we've reached this position, and it doesn't leave one with a clear mind as to what to do next."

"But now I'm home, and after ten minutes I'm starting to feel British again. When I'm away, I try to divorce myself from that. Don't ask me why. I just don't know. I suppose I just want to be Ziggy."

David, since you've been away,

a word called "decadence" has crept into rock, and is now used by every rock riter. And David you have been held to blame for this "decadence."

He smiles.

"Yes . . . er, I can imagine that."

He smiles.

"What do you have to say about it Roy? Am I responsible for it?" he inquires.

Well, I was in the States when YOU happened. I just read in MM that you had arrived, and it was decadent rock. I saw a picture of you, and I thought 'what the . . .'.

Bowie laughs. "Yeah, it was Melody Maker that made me. It was that piece by Mick Watts. I became a performer after that. That's true. It was the first time I had talked to the Press about wanting to come back on stage and be a performer, rather than a writer. During the interview I really saw that I wanted to perform again."

And did you expect it to come this far?

"No. Never. I was a non-performing artist, excited about working on stage again, and well . . . It all exploded."

"We moved at such intensity, such speed. I wrote so quickly. It wasn't until months after that I realised what I'd been writing. When the last period finished I sat back, and went 'wow'. It took the wind totally out of my sails."

But you seem okay. I mean, I think you're very normal.

"Oh, of course I am. I mean this decadence thing is just a bloody joke. I'm very normal. (Conversation is lost in a tunnel.)

"I mean this so called decadent thing happening in English rock. Is it really decadence? Is it what I would call decadence?"

How would you define decadence David?

"Not putting a white rose on a white table for fear of the thorn scratching the table."

I see. I did.

"I don't really feel that decadent rock has arrived . . . yet. It will do."

How do you feel about Roxy Music?

"Well, maybe they are the nearest thing to being decadent at the moment. And I love them."

"I really love them."

"I'm going to buy their new album tomorrow. That's the first thing I'm going to do."

What sort of a person do you find yourself now. You talk of illness, and you want to work harder. (At the Parisian cafe, he told me he had NO death wish). But what are you now?

"I am me, and I have to carry on with what I've started. There is nothing else for me to do. I have been under a great strain though. For me, performing is indeed a great strain. I have also become disillusioned with certain things."

Like what?

"Well, it's very hard to say, but I never believed a hype could be made of an artist before that artist had got anywhere. That's what happened you see. I didn't like it. But when I saw that our albums were really selling, I knew that one period was over. The hype was over. Well, it wasn't, but at least we'd done something to be hyped about. Dig?"

Yes.

"But that whole hype thing at the start was a monster to endure. It hurt me quite a lot. I had to go through a lot of crap. I mean I never thought Ziggy would become the most talked about man in the world. I never thought it would become that unreal.

"I don't want to be studied as a boy next door type character—neither do I want to be thought of as weird. I want to maintain a balance between both.

, "The characters I have written about have indeed been the roles I have wished to portray. Ziggy—that dear creature. I loved him."

"I feel somewhat like a Dr Frankenstein. Although Ziggy follows David Bowie very closely—they are really two different people. What have I created?"

"Ziggy hit the nail on the head. He just came at the rightest, ripest time," he added.

"Dylan once said of writers that they just pluck things from the air, and put them down. Later you can look back on them, and read things into them. I pluck from the air . . . It's only later that I see what I've plucked."

"I know that I appear to write ahead of myself. I mean, let's take "Aladdin Sane." What was written then was written quickly, and really, without much thought as to what it was about."

"But now, I sit back and look at those lyrics, and took at that album, and it's very valid y'know. Sure I have concepts. I have story-lines for the albums, but the actual thought, the actual inspiration comes suddenly, and is written as it comes."

"What keeps me together, what shoulders these 'escapades' of mine is this dear wife that I have. This dear woman Angie, who knows David Bowie . . . ah, she knows me better than I do."

Wherever we travelled, each station, each town, there were few spare minutes when he didn't hug, kiss, and point at his lady, and say, loudly "She's the greatest."

"He gets very evil after a few beers, I mean Roy, look at his face now—he's Jean Genie, he's a little villain, but he's lovely," said Angie, looking after us all. One remarkable woman to be sure.

"It's not a death wish that I have Roy, although the very fact that I say that means that the thought enters my mind. But, y'know we're all very normal . . . And it's about time we told people so."

"Otherwise what those kids are aiming for—I mean the revolution—is going to melt away. It's now we have to revolt. But . . . sensibly . . . and with thought."

Do you feel you are a statesman—or a performer?

"I don't ever want to be a statesman Roy. I am a performer, and I leave space on that stage for theatre too. But a statesman? No. I know only a thin line separates a songwriter from being an entertainer, or making statements. I realise my responsibilities.

"With Ziggy, I became Ziggy on stage. I really was. That was my ego." (This statement followed the entrance and emergence from another tunnel.)

And what is your ego now?

"Strong, and getting fiercer, but I don't think it's Ziggy anymore. It's a more mature David Bowie."

You mean mature as being calmer?

Yes, more aware, more in control of myself. I think that's good. That will keep me alive."

You see I have no idea what I look like on stage. I have never seen a film. I just don't know what I look like when I become 'that thing'. I must see a film of myself. It is essential.

"I can't wait to see what we actually are."

"I know that visually the band is going to be reducing. I mean everyone's wearing make-up aren't they. Eh? We are going to reduce on that level. It will still be David Bowie and The Spiders though."

"I know I have created a somewhat strange audience—but that audience is also full of little Noddy Holders, and Little Iggy Pops. I know we used to attract a load of 'queens' at one stage, but then other factions of people crept in. Now you can't tell anymore. They're all there for some reason."

"And we get young people. Those lovely young people. And they have to be considered very seriously. They cannot be forgotten—as they might be. We cannot afford to lose them by continuing to make rock an intellectual thing.

"We must not leave the young behind. I repeat that."

"You see I don't want to aim statements at them. Again, the whole idea of being a statesman is abhorrent to me."

And then the train stopped. We looked at each other. And it was Charing Cross. He smiled.

Roxy Music's
Andy McKay.
See page 24

Everybody's favourite monster: Alice Cooper.   See page 5

The Year of Outrage

by Chris Charlesworth

Sheer energy has catapulted Slade from Wolverhampton skinheads to the likeliest British cult band of the seventies. And their energy shows no signs of flagging.

They are the most consistent hit singles band in Britain, while their albums too have retained high chart placings months after their original release.

In 1972 Slade arrived, and they're making damn sure they'll be around for the rest of the decade. At their present rate of progress, nothing short of a catastrophe will stop them.

Slade are new, brash and easy to identify with — three essential ingredients for any rock band looking for fame on a wide scale. Their fans are like themselves—a new breed of youngsters searching anxiously for their own heroes instead of those handed down from previous generations.

Slade are like a football team. There's Noddy Holder at centre-half, the sturdy rock of the side on which all their attacks are built; there's Dave Hill, the sprightly inside

forward ready to shoot wherever the slightest opportunity arises; there's Jim Lea, the winger who's at home either in defence or attack and there's Don Powell, the goalkeeper, the last line in defence and a springboard to boot a number right to the back of a hall.

Small wonder that Slade have paralleled themselves with a football side. Their fans chant as if they were saluting goalscoring heroes, they wave scarves in a moving ensemble of red and white that ranks on a par with Liverpool's famous supporters and they break out into "You'll Never Walk Alone", the traditional football anthem, as each Slade concert gets under way.

The allegiance of the fans to Slade is similar to the fierce support that top soccer clubs expect from their fans. Every teenager dreams of becoming a George Best. Now they can dream of becoming a Noddy Holder.

Slade were born about seven years ago in Wolverhampton, where they still live. As so often is the case, the

various members had played in rival amateur groups in the town before coming together. First they were the In Betweens, then Ambrose Slade and now Slade. Apart from a stint in the Bahamas backing soul singers, they didn't really get off the ground until manager Chas Chandler took them under his wing.

Chandler played bass guitar with the old Newcastle group, the Animals, and also discovered and managed Jimi Hendrix. He had a wealth of experience in the music business to draw on to guide Slade's career, a job he has undertaken with resolute efficiency.

It was Chandler's influence that brought about the skinhead look which the group adopted in 1969 at the time of their first minor hit "Shape Of Things To Come". Slade cut their hair and took to wearing boots and braces to appeal to the skinhead cult which was growing up in London and elsewhere. It was a move not unlike the Who's mod image in the mid-sixties, but it failed to pay off with the same results at the time.

As a result Slade became somewhat alienated by bookers on the ballroom circuit who imagined that an appearance by the group would attract the town's skinheads and trouble would inevitably break out. The opposite was more often the case: skinheads who attended a Slade show would be so exhausted by the end of the night that they had no energy left for vandalism at the end of the concert.

The group released an album "Play It Loud" on Polydor, following a change from the Fontana label, and while the record didn't exactly set the world alight Slade were getting more and more club bookings. They worked harder and harder up and down the country to establish an enormous club following. By late 1970, even though their name hadn't been seen much in the charts, a Slade gig was becoming an automatic sell-out.

"Get Down And Get With It", a firm favourite from their stage act, was the turning point. While it didn't sell as much as their more recent singles, it was played on radio and gave the group much needed national exposure. The club fans bought it and the group's popularity accelerated at an alarming rate.

It was only natural that their next two singles—the beginning of the tradition of mis-spelt titles—should be huge hits. They could no longer play clubs as the audiences were growing out of club proportions, and another milestone in the career was reached at the Lincoln Festival last year when they proved they could handle an audience of progressive fans as well as a club audience packed with their own followers.

From Lincoln they went from strength to strength, selling out London's Rainbow Theatre—a gig which attracted the now commonplace Slade queues of silver bowler hatted fans—and selling out their first major British concert tour. Earlier in 1973 they notched up another success by filling the Wembley Empire Pool twice in one day and last summer saw them taking on an 18,000 crowd at the giant Earls Court Arena.

Slade—despite the words of their song—have kept their boots on and it's paid off. From the moment they first put their stomping feet into boots about three years ago, they've been fired by a relentless optimism which has given them confidence to take on the largest of challenges. And now, with a little help from

Chandler, Slade find themselves in a position which could be compared to that of the Rolling Stones a decade earlier.

There's a subtle hint of naughtiness about them—the same underlying villainy that Andrew Oldham pioneered when he launched the Stones. Nice girls loved the Beatles and so did mums and dads. No-one over 25 liked the Stones, and it's pretty doubtful whether Slade appeal to a wholesome audience.

Slade have always been a bit naughty. There was the skinhead stunt at a time when skinheads were put down by all and sundry, and Noddy Holder has come close to being arrested on stage before now for using some pretty colourful language. Their act, too, is blatantly sexy. They urge couples to "feel" each other during slower numbers and build up to an excitement level like working towards a sexual climax.

Holder's sighs, growing louder and more frantic, become an invitation for girls to shudder and scream as if they, too, were enjoying some kind of sexual ecstasy. Small wonder the stage after a Slade concert is littered with bras and panties each bearing a message of invitation.

Football chants, bras, panties, silver top hats and waving scarves serve to set the scene for a concert and combine to form a celebration where the music plays a smaller role than it does with most groups. A Slade show is more an event than a musical evening.

The four young men who make up the group are among the most down to earth of any successful pop musicians. Up until this summer all four members of the band still lived at home with their parents. Only recently did they invest money in houses and expensive cars and they still retain all their links with Wolverhampton. They are very careful about spending money.

As lead vocalist Noddy Holder is the self-elected leader of the group. Holder still retains the skinhead look while the other three have drifted away from boots and braces. It is Holder's slightly evil personality that shapes the group's stage act. He has that enviable talent for communicating with an audience and it is a rare thing if an audience fails to obey his requests from the stage.

Holder also possesses one of the most powerful singing—and shouting —voices in rock. His large round eyes peering out from beneath curly hair and the now familiar top hat give

him a curiously Dickensian look. He could act the part of the archetypal dirty old man with ease—rubbing his hands together and leering out at the girls in the audience.

Lead guitarist Dave Hill—"H" to his friends—is the youngest member of the group and the most energetic on stage. He wears the most outlandish stage clothes of the four and moves around in an ungainly fashion kicking legs and waving his arms around, making a rather incongruous figure. He has a Jensen car with the registration number YOB 1. Like bassist Jim Lea he spends much of the show playing from conveniently placed boxes at the sides of the stage or vaulting up on to speaker cabinets.

Lea is the most serious musician of the four. For several years he played violin in Stafford Youth Orchestra, an experience he demonstrates during his occasional violin number with Slade. He is the only member of the group with any formal musical education, and can also handle a piano with confidence if not virtuosity. His pounding bass work is an essential part of Slade's driving music.

The similarity in sounds between a hard kicked bass drum pedal and a booted foot makes Don Powell's drumming job as demanding as any. Without exception, Slade's singles have relied on a slogging, foot stomping rhythm which Powell, the quietest member of the group, has provided. The enthusiasm which Powell injects into his role often brings him towards total exhaustion by the end of a concert.

Between them, the four who make up Slade have manufactured a rough, raw excitement which was much needed after a comparatively stagnant post Beatles pop singles period.

Opposite:
Slade's
Noddy
Holder

The Year of Outrage
Roxy Music
by Richard Williams

NOVEMBER, 1971: The 100 Club is a jazz cellar on Oxford Street, in the West End of London. Usually its low ceiling trembles to the blare of Trad or Blues, but tonight the place has been rented out for some kind of youth club party.

The audience is full of 13-year-old girls in 20-year-old party dresses, with hoop skirts and rustling petticoats cinched in by wide belts. A ribbon in the hair, no make-up, all the girls dancing together, boys sipping Cokes and nudging each other.

Except for this . . . *creature,* who floats across to the bar. Slinky pencil skirt below the knee, pill-box hat, bright peroxide spiky hair-do, and a good stab at an hourglass figure. Like Jayne Mansfield in a Buster Keaton movie.

The children cast sidelong glances. Who is this person? "She's with the band . . .". Ah.

Something is happening here, and only about seven people know what it is.

Six of them take the stage. They're called Roxy Music, and they're the band. Nothing special to look at, except the lead singer, who sports a green ice-hockey jacket, and the man behind a desk piled with tape-recorders, ring modulators, and other electronic gadgetry, whose long white hair and wan features give him the appearance of a cadaver newly hauled from the Thames.

The singer, seated at an electric piano, mutters something and they begin to play. It's a song about a girl in a car, glimpsed but not forgotten, and the chorus is simply a repetition of the car's registration number, sung by the electronics man and the saxophonist, leaning into their mikes.

"She's the sweetest queen I've ever seen (CPL 593H . . .)"

The sound is like the bastard product of a liaison between the Marcels and one of the heavier German groups. It's not funk, and it's not boogie: it's thunderous and battering, relentless and irresistible.

It sounds like a hit record.

FEBRUARY, 1972: Bingo is the scene most nights at the Granada, Wandsworth Road, London S.W.8. Fruit machines line the foyer, and this afternoon a man with a broom is sweeping up last night's cigarette butts.

Suddenly, a burst of machine-gun guitar raises the dust in the disused balcony, followed by the sound of a rock 'n' roll band gunning its way through a half-remembered song.

"See here she comes see what I mean (CPL 593H . . .)"

The famous manager has come to hear Roxy Music.

There are many ways of getting into the rock biz. Most bands plod on for years in the small clubs, with

25

Roxy Music: Eno, Phil and Andy

a small-time manager, paying their dues and waiting for the break. When the break comes, along with the Sounds of the 70s broadcasts and the Marquee residency, they usually dump the manager in favour of some more experienced career-director. That's how so few managers end up with so many bands.

What Roxy Music are doing is attempting to miss out the primal stage, trying to move in somewhere near the top. They believe that they're good enough not to have to muck about at the bottom end of the scale.

It might seem a bit arrogant. After all, they only got a roadie last week. But John Peel has heard them, and on their first set for Radio One's Top Gear they laid down a set so good that a couple of record companies began to nibble at them. The buzz has started.

On stage at the Granada are Bryan Ferry (vocals, electric piano), David O'List (guitar), Graham Simpson (bass), Andrew Mackay (saxophones and oboe), and Paul Thompson (drums). In the middle of the stalls is the same pile of tape machines, mixers, synthesisers, and other electronic detritus, under the fingers of the pallid Brian Eno.

Ferry and Simpson are the founders, both of them from Newcastle University. Ferry, who studied painting and sculpture with pop-art hero Richard Hamilton, sang with mid-Sixties semi-pro soul bands until he came down to London, where he taught, drove trucks, and exhibited his sculptures. Simpson came south independently, and they met again in 1970 to begin the concept of the present band.

Mackay is a former member of the National Youth Orchestra, and is a teacher. Thompson, like Ferry from County Durham, is one of only two musicians in the band with experience of professional gigging: he's backed Billy Fury, for instance.

The other pro is O'List, former 17-year-old prodigy of the Nice, in the days of "Emerlist Davjack" and "Flower King Of The Flies". He left the Nice in odd circumstances back around '67, and he's been completely silent for five years. Ferry and Mackay remembered his old stuff, decided he was the man they wanted, and spent weeks tracking him down.

Helping Eno to mix the sound is a lad named Philip Manzanera, also a guitarist, formerly with a defunct but very interesting group called Quiet Sun. Venezuela-born, Manzanera met the Roxies at a party and was offered the mixing gig.

The band are playing some of Ferry's compositions, and considering they have a mere 20 gigs (19 of them duff) under their belts, they sound pretty good. O'List curls his guitar phrases out with authority, if a little too much volume, and only the backing vocals lack confidence.

Ferry says he likes Smokey Robinson, Ethel Merman, Marcel Duchamp, Leadbelly, Andy Warhol, and the Velvet Underground, and his songs reflect a wide variety of subjects: "2 HB" is based on Bogart's movie Casablanca, the swirling smoky piano imitating tape-loops, while "Sea Breezes" is a little bit of Brighton Rock mixed up with The Dream of Olwen, featuring dramatic, mournful oboe and wave effects from the synthesiser.

These latter come from Eno, whose antecedents are a little vague. Shall we just say that he has been "prominent" in avant-garde electronic music scenes? And that the discoveries of John Cage, Terry Riley, Morton Feldman, et al are no mystery to him? Yes, except to add that he likes Shep and the Limelites, and once sang with his own rock band, Maxwell Demon.

They play for an hour, more or less continuously, and at the end they go into a huddle with the famous manager. He promises to call them. It's in the air.

"I don't know", says the manager, rolling his battered but comfy Aston Martin back towards Kings Road. "I really don't know".

JUNE, 1972: Eventually, he made up his mind and signed them, and that clinched it. The famous manager, David Enthoven, has a reputation for handling hits—ELP, King Crimson, T. Rex up to and including "Ride A White Swan".

So here we are now at the Greyhound, Croydon, where 500 people can't get in to see David Bowie and the Spiders From Mars because of fire regulations, and Roxy Music are opening the show.

It's the last number:

"I could talktalktalktalktalk myself to death . . . but I believe I would only waste my breath . . . she's the sweetest queen I've ever seen (CPL 593H . . .)"

The final climactic crescendo is swamped with cheers. It's the last number of the set, and it's won over a thousand people.

Roxy look different now: they have various kinds of costumes, from Andy's jump-suit to Phil Manzanera's sci-fi shades . . . wait! Phil Manzanera? Yes, O'List is missing, and Phil pumps out the guitar licks. Yet again, Davey is off the bandwagon.

And there's another change, too: Graham Simpson, co-founder, has gone, after strange events in the recording studio, where they've been working on their first album.

His replacement is a skinny longhair from Nottingham called Rik Kenton, a friend of Pete Sinfield, who's producing the album. Rik's image in the band is . . . well, schoolboyish. You know, the kind that gets accosted on the way to the bus-stop by dirty old ladies.

Later, from the back of the hall, they watch Bowie's billiantly synchronised act. Ferry's eyes are narrowed. He looks like a student at a master class, secreting knowledge.

NOVEMBER, 1972: the first album has been up the charts, and the first single. The capacity crowd at Manchester's purpose-built Hard Rock emporium know all the words off by heart.

As the band comes on stage, burly lads who probably play Rugby League on Saturday afternoons stride around the floor yelling: "Eno, Eno, Eno . . ." The magic of showbiz charisma forever defies logical explanation.

They run through the set, with few mistakes or rough edges, and more adventure in the instrumental sections. Mackay and Manzanera parade their talents in a brilliant neo-Spanish section of "If There Is Something" which brings the house down.

". . . (CPL 593H)"

The Roxies run off stage, waving, blowing kisses, pursued by deafening cheers. They haven't played the single, and the crowd wants it.

Ferry returns, togged up in a Juan Belmonte suit of lights, waspwaisted and sharp at the shoulders (weeks later, it's copied by Gary Glitter).

"Well", says Ferry, "we never expected *anything* like *this*".

Liar.

They perform the single, to general displays of euphoric abandon.

"What's your name? Virginia Plain/ . . ."

A split-second of silence, and then a roar. The roar that greeted Hitler at Nuremburg and Sunderland at Wembley. Blind noise. They've made it, no question.

LATER IN NOVEMBER, 1972: three American rock writers, vacationing in Britain, await Roxy's arrival on the stage of Guildford's Civic Hall.

They're not expecting much, but when the band comes out and goes into the unison "Roxy sway", they're impressed. They're even more impressed by the music, with some reservations. They're absolutely knocked out after the show, when they go backstage and see the little glitter-eyed girls trying to break down the glass door into the dressing-room.

The girls are let in, and quietly wait around for autographs. The Americans drink champagne with the Roxies, and make assignations for interviews.

Yes, they agree, Roxy could do well in the States. It all depends . . .

MARCH, 1973: as it happens, they didn't. The American tour, just before Christmas, did them little good—they were booked to appear with acts like Edgar Winter and Humble Pie, before reds-and-Ripple audiences disinclined to ponder on stylistic nuances. "Here's looking at you, kid", passed over their numbed heads.

So Roxy returned, wiser, and cut another album. Tonight they're premiering some of the songs in a barn-like gym at Nottingham University. They take risks, starting with the new stuff, very much in control.

Kenton has gone, and Bryan's old Newcastle friend John Porter is in his place. Porter, a session musician, has gigged in the States, and his experience pulls them together so that, for the first time, they sound like a real live working road band.

Leaving the new single, "Pyjamarama", to last, they find they've come home to triumph.

APRIL, 1973: the album is already in the British top five, and the group is touring Europe for the first time.

Having covered Italy, they're now in Paris, staying at the incredible George V, planning to nick the monogrammed bathrobes.

An entourage from their management and record company is there to see them conquer the Olympia music hall, which they accomplish with no sweat.

The act is now tight, precise, unyielding. Take it or leave it—and the Parisians take it, avidly, to their hearts.

Afterward's there's a party for 40 people in an old restaurant. Escargots, Burgundy, fresh strawberries, people climbing in and out of windows, bread rolls thrown from table to table. Eno plays with a barrel-organ, while Ferry muses aloud on the subject of his forthcoming solo album.

It's all over, bar America. Ferry's eyes, though, still seek the future, mirroring his disengaged air. Without coldness, they look inside, in every second a dozen computations and calculations. Over the past couple of years he's used people, discarded some and retained others, and through them achieved every single aim, with interest.

In every dream home, a heartache?

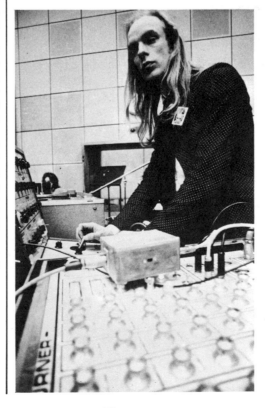

Eno, the wan-faced electronics wizard who quit Roxy in July

The Year of Outrage

Lou Reed

by Michael Watts

Let's recall this night in March at the Alice Tully Hall in Lincoln Center. Despite the foulness of the evening they have come out in droves —the admirers, the scene-makers and the plain curious—to see exactly how the new, refurbished Lou Reed shapes up. The hall is full. Warhol and Morrissey have flown in specially to be backstage. And Fred Heller, his manager, is floating around the auditorium like a hot-air balloon, telling everyone "Louis is going to be **big** in this business".

It is understandable. After all, this **is** New York, where it all began for the Velvets six years ago. Welcome home the prodigal son after six months in England and two years in oblivion. Welcome back, period, from wherever it was. The evening bears all the hallmarks of a Greenwich Village Messiah riding into the promised land to hosannas from Max's Kansas City denizens.

During his first number, some girl hands him a bouquet of flowers. It happens again later on. Would these zealots have anointed his feet with unguents if they hadn't been shod in silver wedgies? His face throughout bears the droll deadpan of a young Jack Benny. *The affection of these children!* He picks up the first bouquet and holds it out to someone in the wings with the vaguely embarrassed expression of having plucked the flowers himself from a window box he'd passed on the way.

But he finally looks the part. The first time in England had been at David Bowie's concert at the Festival Hall. Two songs, right at the end. Dolled up in spangled costume and eyeliner. Something wasn't right. Now the curls have lengthened, the face looks suitably waxy and wacked-out, and the clothes are raunchy: black leather trousers and short jacket, with a black tee-shirt underneath. The paunch has slimmed out.

He uses a four-piece band—two alternate leads, bass and drums— and although they are a little too slicked up and rehearsed for the dramatic intimacy he needs, the playing is fine. The very best moments occur when the tempo shoots up, one or other of the leads rips into a solo, and Lou just stands there, shifting slightly on the balls of his feet with the rhythm guitar grinding out chunks. There's the bleached-out, arid voice, perfectly suited to the tense, claustrophobic rhythm of "Waiting For My Man". And he encores with "Sister Ray". That marvellously funny chorus line of "he's sucking on my ding dong", arch and irresistible.

But there's something still not . . . Finally, I think I figure it out. There's a quality about Lou Reed which anchors him too firmly to the sixties, and the Now generation has since moved on. Perhaps some essential songs haven't survived well as lyrics—those songs about addiction, the Warhol oeuvre, naughty New York. They seem as passe now as Max's, home of decadent elitism, with which they came to be associated. In the context of the reasonably cultist audience the Velvets enjoyed they had meaning. Now, when Lou is being promoted as a superstar, there's an element of contrivance and self-consciousness.

Now all this I was thinking three months ago, before I was aware that the 70s had their own Now

generation who want to put Lou Reed into the charts and make him a bona fide pop star. It's only honest that I mention it, even if I don't say it directly to Lou, who at this point in time is looking through the English charts, a flicker of life animating the pale face as he plots a course through the album and singles positions.

"A number one hit? Really?" he queries his new manager, who is currently swopping law suits with Mr. Heller—he was the one who said Louis was going to be big, big, big, of course. Hey, babe, take a walk on the wild side.

It pays off. Two fingers of Scotch in hand, large, brown shades disguising a sleepless night spent writing songs, Louis seems as reasonably pleased with life as his downbeat, turned down stance will allow.

In fact, as the two fingers dwindle to a fingertip some kind of thawing process takes place, which enables him to express proper vituperation suitably laced with cynicism, at the vagaries of critical and commercial success. I'm referring, naturally, to the old adage that the more popular you become the less the critics like you; or, as Lou puts it, "the two are hand in glove, and I've watched the critical praise go out the window".

We could name names, of course, but we won't—at least, I won't. "They assume you to be their own little cult figure, and I'm nobody's cult figure", he says. They ask me, "are you selling out, are you trying for mass appeal now?" But I tell ya, the vast bulk of Velvet Underground fans have stuck with me through all our RCA escapades". A swift snort of disgust. "I don't give a damn what they think".

Don't expect him, either, to be overjoyed at the constant repetition of Bowie's name. Not that they aren't compadres any more, just that he's had it up to here with the suggestion that they were climbing on each other's backs to get where they are: the whole Master/Disciple relationship, in fact.

"It was a lotta fun", he answers slowly and precisely. "I had fun and I think David did. I never thought of the relationship like that. I know David has said things like that, but I don't believe it. I haven't seen him for a long while. I don't know what he was up to, I don't honestly know.

"I think people buy things if they like it, and if they don't they won't But I'm so tired of being linked with

it. It had positive and negative aspects, and I'm sure both of us would prefer if it was said, 'enough'. He deserves what he's got. His songs, they were good songs, much better than other people's, I think."

Tony DeFries? "Aw", a wave of the scotch glass, "he was always running around telling people he was my manager, which he wasn't, although he tried".

Let's talk of London—where it all started again after two years spent in and out of court: aftermath of the Underground. All that glitter at the Festival Hall, he recalls . . . well, he only had this one suit available, and that was it. And by the way, he didn't think all that stuff· was shit, by any means.

"I switch characters all the time", he notes dryly. "I only did three or four shows like that, and then it was back to leather. We were just kidding around."

He didn't write a single song all the time he was in London. I put it to him that whatever he had written would have had a much different perspective to what was composed in New York. In essence, he was tied to New York by an umbilical chord. His writing was as New York in its own way as that of Damon Runyon's, and to envisage a Damon Runyon transplanted to any other city was somehow unthinkable.

He agreed, but pointed out that elements of life found in New York also existed in London. He'd personally found life a little slow-paced there towards the end of his stay, but he knew a whole lot of people from the old New York scene who had made their homes there, like Pat Hartley (who appeared in the Hendrix film, "Rainbow Bridge").

"She's now got a baby", he remarks, tugging at his glasses. "Probably puts amphetamine in its food."

After I'd laughed and he'd smiled wanly, I said if that wasn't a comment that only a New Yorker would make: sardonic humour, fast on the lip. You have to maintain a certain cynicism in a city where internecine warfare is being conducted daily.

Inevitably, the conversation turns towards the darker side of New York life. He refuses to accept that there's anything low-life in his writing or associations with the old New York scene. Bowie himself had suggested that this aura of decadence —an increasingly trite word—was mostly part of the image-making that surrounded the two of them. True or false?

"Well", and he puts on that tired, pained look, "there are some people who'd say I'm definitely supposed to be, and then there are others who're much more decadent than me. Y'know, what does decadence mean?" A shrug of the shoulders. "Is it the connotation of bisexuality and drugs? David's never been associated with drugs, but me, I've always been accused of it. I wrote 'Heroin', right? You got to write about what you see and know, else someone who does know says it's a crock of shit. And no-one has said that about me. It's all this, except that sometimes I'm detached —it's not about me personally."

But wasn't he still writing about the same topics as seven years ago?

"Are you doing what you did in '66? Huh? You refine it and polish it off in '73."

The subject, he says, that currently interests him most is suicide. Not just that Warhol star Andrea Whips threw herself out of a window and hit the sidewalk so hard her footprints are still there, no, because it's kind of "exciting".

"Have you ever stood at a window and seen the pavement, and thought, "just what would happen if I leaned forward a foot?" Then you'd find out if there was a heaven and a hell. Sometimes you get things out of people's systems by writing and performing a song about that. But that's not the reason I do what I do. One of my ideas was to introduce these people here in New York to others who aren't in contact with that kind of experience, and in a very simple way—by record. They just meet them through me, and if they don't like them they can always take the needle off".

But wasn't there a degree of negativity about what he was doing?

He looks vaguely disgusted. "The Beatles never had anything to say. It was always nice, happy stuff. What did they ever say?" This thought seems to work him up a little.

"Lennon has been trying recently, but he's involved in a New York scene that was dead seven years ago, hanging around with people like Jerry Rubin." He takes off his glasses. "I don't really like people telling me what to do and pushing for peace and whatever. I say bull shit. My approach is, why don't we get down to what's really going on? The greatest thing about the Velvet Underground was its honesty."

As we'd touched on the subject of low-life themes in pop music I mentioned Zappa. This provoked dislike bordering on vindictiveness.

"I say this although he admires me, I may add, which doesn't impress me a bit. I know I'm good. He thinks he's good. He couldn't write a decent song if you gave him a million and a year on an island in Greece". He drew breath. "And if you want to hear pretentiousness, just listen to John Lennon's 'Imagine'. All that 'possessions' shit."

If you think Lou is any more kindly disposed towards the new breed of New York underground bands, then you're mistaking him. He doesn't believe that any of them are going to happen: "It's going to die before it starts. Why? Because it's derivative, but also it's talentless. Half of them are from California, anyway."

Still, he has a soft spot for Max's. It's still the only place to go, even if in its heyday you couldn't get in the door without being checked out if you were suitable; these days they take anybody. He hasn't been in quite a while.

"Hey, we're talking about Max's!" he calls to his manager. "And Mick Ruskin (the owner). He's fabulous. He helped me a lot. In the old days if you were trying to achieve something he'd let you sign tabs, knowing he wouldn't get it back, just so's you'd get to eat. Then again, we drew in a lot of people for him!" He looks at his Scotch, which now contains another two fingers.

New York, he explains, has changed, though not really. Drugs, fashion, sexuality—the preoccupations of the old underground—have simply emerged into the daylight. "Max's is still the place to go if you're into the same old things."

A lot of the old people are missing, though. Take Nico, now in Paris with her husband, Philippe. Hasn't done a thing since her film with Pierre Clementi, "La Cicatrice Interieure".

He tugs at the whisky. "Nico was a star in her own universe. Anyone who comes into contact with her will never be the same. If you don't know her, she doesn't talk much, but if you do . . . wow. She is brilliant, I adore her and her songs. When I ask people over to my house and play records I always work up towards her songs. She can have an effect on you."

Warhol, I said, was now a massive socialite. Every time you opened Women's Wear Daily he was featured.

Well, he replied, a few years ago he had been twice as big a celebrity. He had gone through that socialite scene himself. He knew a lot of the people.

Candy Darling, Sugar Plum, Little Joe—none of them had minded a bit about "Walk On The Wild Side". Candy now wanted to make a record, "Candy Darling Does Lou Reed". She knew all the words. Strictly speaking, "he" is a "she", of course.

Everything is pretty much all right these days with Lou Reed barring the odd lawsuit and critic. He looks very expensive, and his manner borders on the expansive, for him. He's married to a girl named Betty, who has short, blonde hair and seems normal enough to be somebody's sister. A lot of people in New York didn't like it when they were united in holy matrimony; they'd typed him as a closet queen.

Sometimes Lou used to panic when he thought the old writing touch had deserted him, but then he came to realise it doesn't go away for ever. It took him a long time to learn that, though. What could he have done? Got into journalism school?

"I don't know how to do anything else", he says. It's probably true.

The Year of Outrage

Elton John

by Chris Welch

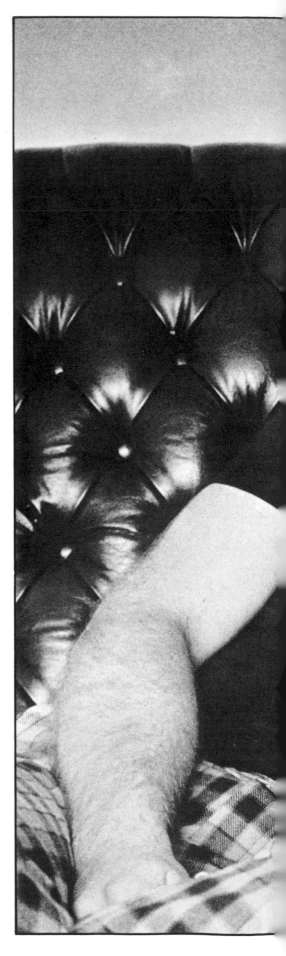

Set among a warren of screened villas on a private estate, Elton John's pad is a jewel of neatness, and spare good taste. There is no clutter. Beautiful objects are enhanced by lighting, setting and space. From the neatly folded face flannel in the marble bathroom ("most expensive in the world, built by Wimpeys of London"), to the suit of armour guarding the stairway, all is a kind of tidy perfection one would expect to see at the Ideal Home Exhibition, and doesn't. In fact Elton's house makes the Ideal Home Exhibition look like a display of Nissen huts shortly before demolition by squads of sanitary engineers.

It seemed almost offensive to flick cigarette ash into the glittering ash trays, but MM photographer Barrie Wentzell made us all feel at home by instantly pouring champagne upon the carpet. We sat and watched Elton sponge down the hand embroidered rug (delivered by courier from Baghdad after a murderous overland journey of seven weeks), with quiet sorrow.

"It's all right," he said.

"We're terribly sorry."

"That's all right." Elton squeezed Dom Perignon and scrubbed more vigorously. He is used to such accidents, as a man who had some 250 guests over for a party complete with drag act and strippers.

"Donovan's having a party next week, and he's invited the whole world. It threatens to be a booze up. Keith Moon says he doesn't want any galactic fairy dust, he wants a good booze-up. Rod says he's not much into mushrooms and toadstools, but he'll go."

As can be gathered, rock celebrities are among his near neighbours and he says: "I had trouble insuring the house because we live too near Keith Moon! I was going to buy his house originally. Then I saw a picture of Keith in the *Mirror*, outside the place, and I knew it was too late. I was going to buy another house called Charters Farm. When I saw the owner I called it Farters Charm . . . by mistake of course. I've lived here for a year now and before that I lived in London, only five minutes from the Speakeasy. I never got any sleep for years."

Apart from a swimming pool, one of the more pleasing diversions about the house is a games room, complete with genuine jukebox, stocked by Elton with hits by Judge Dread, Rod Stewart and T. Rex; a musical pin-table, and a football game at which Elton is such an expert

he gave the MM a 9-0 thrashing.

Yet amid all these splendours there is one possession that gives him most pleasure, a suitcase full of spectacles of varied hues and designs. "This really freaks out the customs." But, without them, he cannot see much farther than the end of his grand piano.

The piano, big and black, takes up one corner of the main lounge, and Elton avows that he never plays his own compositions on it. "I just doodle. Great fun doodling."

His tastes in music are wide, ranging from the classics to David Cassidy. "Poor guy. I know him quite well. We took him to the Troubador in LA to see a group and it was the first time he had been out in one-and-a-half years. He'll keep up the pace for a while then go and live in Hawaii for the rest of his life.

"You know he gets up at 6 am every day, goes to the TV studio, makes an LP, gives a concert—he's like a robot. He gets very depressed. He asked Bernie and I to write a song for his next album, and I wouldn't mind that at all. People like him always get written off. Because it's the Osmonds for example everybody says: 'Oh it's terrible.'

"But records like 'Crazy Horses', are really good. It's a sign of everybody getting old when they start grousing about the groups. The trouble is, there are no young groups around today. All the 'new groups' are the same old faces coming back

again."

We talked about his album "Don't Shoot Me I'm Only The Piano Player", which could perhaps be some kind of answer to the Mailbag blues.

"We made the LP in June 1972 and it seemed like it would never come out. But I wanted a long gap and we only had one LP out in '72. I didn't want the situation where every few months there was an Elton John album out.

"My first five albums were released in the first three weeks of my career. Yes, it was a hurried job. I prefer to have the situation where you have a hit LP and have another already in the can. Before, everytime we went into the studio it was a rush. Two days to go and he hasn't written the songs yet! This one was done in France when I was on my last legs. I had glandular fever, which I never had before. The first day in the studio, I said to Gus (Dudgeon), 'I can't make the album'.

"I felt it had more balls than the previous albums. I haven't got the voice to sing ballsy songs—it's a drag. I'd love to stand there and scream.

"It was more of a band album. It's better than just Elton John and his f——— piano," Elton laughed. "Legs Larry's told me some marvellous things you can do with a piano. But I just put mine through a Leslie Speaker cabinet.

"It took me over a year to find out

how to amplify the piano. I use nine ordinary microphones and it took my roadie a year-and-a-half working on it. I've tried the most incredibly complicated contact mikes you have to pin on separately, and they've made the piano sound like an electric piano. It's very hard to get a natural sound.

"I do play the piano at home, I've hardly written anything at home. I always forget my words. I can't remember anything from the first LP, neither can Bernie. I can't remember the chords. Songs are like pints of milk. You drink one, like it, then want another one.

"We used to play 'Whole Lotta Shakin' on stage for an ending, but that gets boring and we got fed up playing it. They asked me to play on Jerry Lee's album, but I said no. He was so disappointing when I saw him at the Palladium, and as far as I'm concerned he was the best rock and roll pianist ever.

"I thought it was going to be a gas. I went in me drape jacket and got jeered at by the Teds. He could have wiped the audience out, but he just sat there and played country and western numbers as if to say 'F——you.' All those old rock stars are the same."

If Elton is critical of his erstwhile heroes, he can be equally self-critical. "When I played at Crystal Palace in 1971 I came out and played acoustic numbers for an hour and bored everybody. I knew I had

played badly and everybody said I had played badly."

"They're funny—my LPs. When I think about them, they're a bit like Beatles albums. I mean—just ten songs. I'd like to have more of the band featured, more improvisation. We improvise a lot more on stage now. But mainly it's music to drive cars by. I don't know how to evaluate my music. Does this sort of thing appeal to Led Zeppelin fans? It's very strange. I don't think I'm a great player by any means."

But surely Elton had paid his dues as a blues player in the old Marquee days . . . ?

"No, I was useless. I was a vamper. I played on a Vox Continental—until it died. It was a bright red beast, and one day it exploded. I used to think they were great because Alan Price played on one with the Animals. And I'm terrible on Hammond organ. It's too big for me and I'm too lazy to learn about drawbars. I'm not electrically minded at all."

If blues and barrel house were not Elton's forte, were the classics more of an influence?.

"I prefer orchestral stuff to piano music, and I prefer Mahler to Chopin. But when I listened to the 'Elton John' album again recently, it seemed so classically influenced.

"Everything is getting looser now, and we are recording much more quickly than we were in '71. I'd like to experiment a bit more, but

the danger is if I experiment too much, it would be a bastard to reproduce and we'd need another fifteen people on stage. F—— it, we'll use a backing track like the Monkees!"

As a fully established veteran of the rock scene, did he still enjoy the business? "Oh yes, there are so many good bands around. I love black music and always have done. And there is so much more good music around now. Have you heard Stevie Wonder's new album! . . . it's amazing.

"I'm getting a bit fed up with singer-songwriter records. They drive me mad. I was labelled a singer-songwriter, and did four LPs in that syndrome. But I've always fought against the 'Elton John' syndrome. People take it too seriously. I'd like us to be a band. On the first albums we used a lot of session men, but we could never do it that way now, planning it down to the last flute.

"I'm still going to be touring.

"I'd like to play places like the Boston Gliderdrome again. It will be like the old days of revolving stages when the band comes on playing 'I Can't Turn You Loose', all ferreting about for a microphone lead."

"I never get to see many concerts myself. But I went to see Alice Cooper in the States and it was incredible, with the helicopter, the shower of panties, the fireworks, it was the best produced show I've ever seen. Really amazing.

"I was caught up in it myself, scrambling for a pair of panties, and the band was so tight. You can't do anything like that over here. You'd get jobsworths backstage saying: 'You can't do that here, who's going to clean up the mess?'

"But the scene is loosening up a bit. The musicians have got over the bit where they say nothing. People talk to audiences now. James Taylor is funny and has got over that shy bit. And Kris Kristofferson is really funny."

There are one or two places in the world that Elton does not find funny however. "I would never work in France. I don't think I sell in France. I sell more records in the Lebanon than I do in France.

"The first time we played together was in France and they booed and threw cabbages at us. Norman Granz was the promoter and he was really upset, and French people kept coming up in tears and apologising for their people.

"I stuck it out for half an hour, and came off to let the star go on. It was Sergio Mendes, and I thought, oh well, he'll go down a storm. But no. He went on and . . . BOO! It's the French way of enjoying a night out. They throw everything at you . . . cigarette packets, knickers, pictures of the Victoria and Albert Museum. But I'm not against the French. I love their food, wine and Paris."

In one year he toured Europe, America, Japan, and Australia. "I turned up like a plate of jelly on the doorstep after that. It's true, I was over-worked! But the truth is we were so knocked out that people wanted us, we said yes to everything. But when you get there, you're so tired, you don't want to do it. So that's why we cooled it in '72."

Elton's least pleasant experiences were in Australia. "When we got there, we were invited to a reception by the Dean of Perth. We were so tired after the flight we rang him and asked if we could make it the next day. Fine. That night on TV there's a big story: 'Elton John snubs the Dean of Perth. He says he was in a mood.'

"Can you dig it? Everything is controversial, even Coronation Street. They have a sign flashing on the screen during the show—'Not suitable for children.' They are so archaic, and they hate the English. Or at least the press hate us. We're still 'Limey bastards' to them. Since

I found that out, I have willed every Australian team to lose.

"My cousin lives there and he had to accept the principles of a beer drinking idiot to survive. Don't worry, they already know what I think about them. When I go back they will be waiting for me. It was a nightmare being there. We played at one football stadium, two race tracks and a speedway track—and it was in the middle of winter. The stage blew away on one gig and we literally played in overcoats. It was raining on the piano. But we'll go back. Why not?

"New Zealand is nice, though. It's like England years ago. It's lovely and green and the people are great. But Australia . . . the band had five days off in Adelaide and they went mad with boredom. If Mary Hopkin can run into trouble there, well it gives you some idea.

"What they need is a tour by Led Zeppelin, the Who and the Faces . . . together. The country would grind to a halt."

As the sun began to set over the swimming pool, Elton drew the many yards of curtains across the picture window, switched on the multi-coloured ball of glass fronds, and inquired if we had heard the funniest, saddest and most excruciating tape ever recorded, the legendary Troggs Tape.

"This was made while the Troggs were recording for their next hit single. The engineer left the tape running and since then everybody has been demanding a copy tape."

We listened to the Troggs, hit making group of some five or more years ago, struggling to communicate with each other in a welter of oaths and broad dialect and missed drum beats.

It has been calculated that a certain four letter word is used nearly 138 times in about ten minutes, and it all proved too much to bear. A hearty meal of beans on toast was summoned, the last dregs of champagne swilled, and it was time to bid adieu. We left Elton dancing to the strains of Stevie Wonder's "Superstition".

The original honky cat.

The Giants Rock On

Led Zeppelin

by Roy Hollingworth

The noise cajunked, and beefed outwards, filling each corner of the circular, space-aged Nassau Coliseum, Long Island, New York State.

Sixteen thousand people didn't know whether they were coming or going. Many danced, crazily, while others just stood, stared and smiled.

Led Zeppelin had been off stage four times. Four times they had fled under the archway to the side of the stage, and four times an unnatural din of screaming and cheering and unbelievable begging had brought them back out.

Now their set was approaching four hours in length—four incredible hours of the most wonderful music. Jimmy Page was on his toes, shaking and trying to pull out a last batch of magical notes. He'd pulled so many that evening, it seemed inconceivable that he could maintain such a peak. But something tricked him, and he spun round, ran across to Robert Plant, bursting, and slamming chords. Plant smiled, threw his head back, and the band rocked so hard you'd have thought there was no tomorrow.

It was one of the most amazing concerts I'd seen from any band, at, any time. Nothing had gone missing, it had been the complete act. There had been power, climax after climax, beauty, funk, rock, boogie, totally freaked passages, and such constant, snarling energy that on this evening Led Zep could have provided enough human electricity to light half of America.

Does anybody really know how big Led Zep are?

So you'll get reports of English bands doing "well" in America, and the reports will be long. You'll hear The Stones, Elton John and The Faces before you hear of Led Zep. Somehow somebody forgot Led

Zeppelin when they were writing home.

And yet for four years Zep have been slaying America. For four years they have met with the doomy criticism that they could never do as well again, and yet they've come back, and done better.

The people know it. The scenes are just ridiculous. Auditoriums and halls are being sold out without any advertising.

Strange how the Zep became unfashionable back home. Sure, they sell albums, and they can fill the Empire Pool—but where were all the trimmings, where was the real flash, the excitement? It was in the audience to be sure, but for some reason the media took it all with a pinch of salt. That Led Zeppelin are possibly the biggest band in the world never figured. And that's a sad mistake.

It figures here, mind. Here Zep are truly recognised. Why do you think they come so often? Money, sure . . . But also because Zep are a band that love playing, and here there are no inhibitions. They find their audience. Here they play their best.

"The scenes have possibly amazed you," said John Paul Jones. "But this has been happening for four years now. I think we all feel a bit annoyed that nobody really knows it back home. Do they really know what we're doing?"

This feeling is common within the band. Why, you might say, should they worry? They do well, the audience—which is the main thing—knows just how big they are. Why should they bother about wee small England and its fickle ways?

Well they're English, and like most people, they also have egos. They'd just like England to know what they're doing.

"Our egos have been hurt," says

Rob Plant.

"They really have. For some reason English critics have never told the truth about us. For some reason they've been out to get at us a bit. So things are clouded over, and nobody gets to know what's really happening. There's been so much bullshit printed it's just untrue.

"We read pages on some band—name not mentioned—saying just how big they are here. You ask the people here just how big they are. We know. You see it makes the English press look ridiculous. It's so annoying," added Jones. "Here we are slaving away, and getting consistently incredible reactions and nobody back home can care anything about us." He shook his head. "It's just not right."

Don't get the idea that Zep are just peeved little boys, with a chip on their shoulders. It's not a case of that at all. It's not a case of them having their own ideas as to how big they are. That position can be seen in a matter of seconds over here. Zep are ace—there are no two ways about it.

"Maybe," said Plant, "if we were as big in England as we are here, I wouldn't be able to walk down a bloody street without being stopped," he laughed. "Don't know if I'd like that or not."

The Scene was The Waldorf Astoria Hotel, on a sickening, heavy, hot New York day. Manager Peter Grant was stood with two house detectives in a corridor. His huge frame dwarfed them somewhat. There had been some trouble over the amount of people visiting Bonzo Bonham's room, and, as per usual, a hotel had it in for longhairs.

The night before had seen the band play the first of two concerts at Nassau. They were overjoyed at

how it had gone.

"Something has really happened this time," said Plant. "Something has really clicked. It's fantastic, the spirit within the band is just fantastic."

Plant is a cheery character, forever jigging, and rocking around, spreading a laugh or two with the first colourful Brummie accent I've ever heard. Talk centred on football.

Page was quietly going about his business, and then in a fit of laughter Bonzo appeared. The grizzly King Drummer. An honest lad who likes to swing sticks like fury, and drink at about the same pace.

"Y'um wouldn't believe what bloody trouble goin' on with my room." It appears that trouble forever surrounds dear Bonzo.

Pretty soon the line of limousines was poking its way in and out of the absurd traffic towards Long Island. The three cars were in radio contact with each other, and the state of traffic soon decreed that somebody's house could not be visited. "Make sure the spare ribs are driven to the Coliseum," came a message over the radio.

Now the Coliseum is a strange building. It sits seemingly in the middle of nowhere, looming like a space research centre, circular and concrete.

Why didn't they play the Madison Square?

"Because it cost 5,300 dollars to book that place," says Peter Grant, "and that's just absurd. This is a great place, and this is where the kids live. Shame there aren't places like this in England. It's getting absurd over there now. There's nowhere to play.

"You know I wanted to put the band on at Waterloo Station. You know, that massive area before the platforms. I thought it was a great idea—you know we could have Led Zeppelin specials coming in on the platforms. It was going to work, but the station authorities said there was one late train that would get in the way. Shame, it would have been great, imagine Led Zep playing Waterloo Station—a completely covered hall, and good accoustics."

They've got a nice PA there.

The Coliseum was beginning to fill, and when I walked out with Plant he was met with a load of handshakers.

"Just want to say you're the best band in the world. You just are. I just want to say that," said one lad. "Ta very much," said Plant, and gave the boy a back-stage pass. "You're the best band in the world," said another. And they really meant it.

Martin, one of the famous crew of Led Zep roadies, was squeezing Plant's lemons in the dressing room. A half-dozen lemons, mixed with honey and tea to feed the Plant voice. How it kept going that night was amazing.

Bonzo was just carrying his sticks, and the clothes he'd arrived in. "I got stopped backstage somewhere you know, and they wouldn't believe I was with the band. They said, where's your stage clothes. I said where's me what? . . ."

The time was right, and the band made it's way out of the room, and stood in a large hall backstage. The excitement just round the corner was thick as 16,000 people made ready. There was that hum, that frightening hum.

An electrical tone was started. It sounded like the rising drone of a bomber. It got louder, louder, till it filled the whole place, and then the band walked onto the stage. The place collapsed, and the band without hesitation kicked into rock.

Page stabbed out a riff, and Plant yelled and squealed, and glory, all Hell broke lose.

Page is the complete guitarist. He captures every emotion that sears through his head, and channels it through his arms. Whether it be a chord, a riff, or a gaggling neckful of notes, he is perfect.

And when technical ability might just swamp feeling, Page finds a dirty dischord, and lets it cut ugly and messy through the tapestry. It sort of jerks your body and throws you, and then he finds a true line again, and weaves on in a straight, sharp direction. Their music has indeed got better. There appears to be a deal more open ended excitement about the unit.

Page is in fine fettle, swaying on his heels, and then shaking his mass of hair into a blurr of tangles, which are picked up by the many spots and turned gold, and then white. Plant gets all very sexual, and mouths, heaves and sighs, and frenzied spluttering down the mike . . . And then he forces that screaming voice right out, Page ends the riff, Bonzo falls silent, Jones stops, and only Plant's crazy voice assaults the silence.

Three acoustic numbers give people time to breathe, lie back and relax. John Paul Jones exhibited a new electric mandolin, that gave a good colourful feel to songs written on Welsh hillsides.

Then they all upped and left dear Bonzo.

He remained, and delivered the most wrecking drum solo you'd ever imagine. He beat the things so hard, with sticks and hands that I thought his arms were going to fall off, or maybe the kit would shatter. His object was to reach grumbling thunder, and that he did, a sort of crazy stampede of drums and sharp,

slashed cymbals. It went on over 15 minutes and he wouldn't stop.

Bonzo would cool it all down to just one motion—he was leaving out what was already bopping in everyone's heads. Everyone knew what Bonzo was playing, but he wasn't playing it—if you can see what I mean.

And then he struck back, and with no nerves at all just smacked everything till it hurt, and hurt. The tempo doubled, and doubled again, and his anguished face and black hair was wet through and streaked with burning sweat.

His final crescendo was just not true. I stood and shook my head in disbelief as he panned everything in sight. Toil and troubles, it just hubbled and crumpled out in a monstrous form. Peter Grant was shaking his head too, and Jim Page, who had snuck back onto the side of the stage, was also staring with admiration at Bonzo. It exploded in one mass of fire and flesh, and Page jumped into view again, and played with his buddy.

The Coliseum just couldn't understand it. They got up and for five solid minutes applauded Bonzo. It was heartwarming, it almost made you want to cry, such was the emotion about, such was the pleasure, and enjoyment of applauding something that had been so incredible.

"Someone once asked me what technicalities I applied to my playing," Bonzo had said to me. "I said technicalities, what the hell are you going on about? I said this is my technicality, and raised my hand into the air, and let it fall. Head to drum, that's what it is, head to drum.

"I'm not trying to be any superstar. I just do my bit as one quarter of Led Zeppelin. When I have a solo I don't ever imagine drummers around watching me. I don't try and impress people who play the drums. I play for people. I don't try and perform the most amazing changes in tempo, or make people watch me. I just couldn't do that—it would take away the essence of Jimmy's guitar, and Robert's voice. John Paul and myself lay down a thick back-drop, that's what we do."

The place was in a fever now of sheer adulation. It couldn't stop, and it didn't. The band stonked into "Whola Lotta Lovin'," with Pagey experimenting bizarrely with the reverb unit. He stood there, on his own, slashing and playing loud. The chords were held in the amps, and then shot out with echo, just as he hit another. Then he took a cello bow, and scraped and banged it across the strings.

Now we're backstage, and the band have run off, but Bonzo's saying they've got to do another, and the screaming is really painful on the ear from outside.

John Paul Jones takes the stage on his own, and sits at an organ. From that he delivers a medley of songs, some old, some new, some forgotten, and then into spine-chilling religious chords.

Soon all the band were back on stage, and Page laid a boogie out, and Plant growled "Boogie Mama," and what a boogie it was. It was like some stoked-up train belting on into the night—Bonzo being the pistons, Page the driver, it gouged into everybody's head.

Things were coming fast and furious. Next thing you know they're into "Peggy Sue," and rock 'n' roll medley. And America goes wild, and dances.

So now we're into the limousine again and Plant is shaking his head. "They'd never believe how good it is here back home. They'd just never believe what happened tonight."

43

The Giants Rock On

Brian Wilson

by Richard Williams

Los Angeles — Wheeling down Beverly Glen Boulevard from Coldwater Canyon in a yellow Checker cab, the desirability of the residences increases almost every quarter-mile.

The stilt-houses jutting out of the Canyon's sides give way to expensive ranch-style bungalows `and mock-Georgian mini-mansions, their hedges trimmed down to just 18 inches, so that passers-by can stare in envy at the Lincoln Continental, the Mercedes coupe, and the kids' twin Stingrays. Gardeners fuss over the flower-beds, surrounded by lawns which look like they're trimmed by nail-clippers, daily.

Make a right turn at the bottom of Beverly Glen, on to Sunset Boulevard, past the baroque pink elegance of the Beverly Hills Hotel (where workmen are, at this moment, retouching the equatorial-forest murals in miles and miles of corridor —by hand, with little brushes and pots of paint), and in a couple of minutes you enter Bel Air.

"Well," says the cab-driver in his sailor hat. "I've been working in L.A. for eight years, and I've been inside here maybe twenty times." Cab-drivers, especially American, don't impress easily. Right now, this one is impressed.

Bel Air is a residential estate, the quintessence of gracious living, Hollywood style. Whereas the board members of Beverly Drive are anxious to show you how far they've come, status-wise, the chairmen up in Bel Air will go to considerable lengths to keep the peekers away.

Just inside the East Gate of the estate, a clean white prowl car lurks

behind some bushes. The foliage, a dazzling early-spring green, thickens along Bellagio Road until all that's visible of the houses is a nest of brick chimneys, or the glint from a leaded window.

Bellagio is the main artery of Bel Air, running from east to west and numbering into the thousands. It's where Brian Wilson lives.

The tension started when I got to the gate, and looked beyond it to the low greenish house, built in the Thirties for Tarzan's creator, Edgar Rice Burroughs. It was quiet—nothin' shakin' but the leaves on the trees.

On the gatepost, a sign said that the house was protected by some patrol or other (I remembered the cabbie's instruction: "You better watch out, all them Bel Air people

got German Shepherds'') and beside it was an intercom grille, with a buzzer-button and the legend: STAND BACK! SPEAK NORMAL.''

It seemed like a good motto for the occasion.

I pressed the buzzer, stood back and waited until Brian's wife Marilyn activated the electric gate-opener. Actually, the gate turned out to be busted and open anyway.

The drive, The front door. Hello Marilyn. The dark hall. Hello Dog, Hello second dog. The living room. Hello third dog. Hello Cat. Hello Diane (Marilyn's sister) Hello . . .

Brian was lying on his front, almost under a big pool table. Diane bent over him, wielding a small electric massage appliance around the back of his neck and the tops of

his shoulders. He was wearing an old red and white shirt outside tatty blue jeans, and battered brown indoor moccasins.

"Brian, this is Richard," said Marilyn.

"Uhh, hi," said Brian, trying to screw his head round and back to see me. He failed, because his long hair fell across his eyes so he gave up and faced the carpet again. "I'm sorry, but I woke up this morning, and I had this . . . uh . . . . headache. Can't get rid of it . . real bad."

Okay, I told myself. Perch on the pool table and talk with Marilyn. Stand back, speak normal.

I wanted to hear the new (American) Spring material Diane and Marilyn had just finished cutting, with Brian's help, in Iowa. Why Iowa? Seems they had a friend there, and the friend had a friend with a studio, and more friends who're musicians, and one thing led to another.

It was snowing in Iowa (it's in the 70s in L.A.) but Brian looked round again to say that it's the best studio he's ever used. They had a great time, using unknown musicians and working hard.

Marilyn got out the copy tape of the sessions, and played me four completed tracks over the new set of JBL studio monitor speakers suspended from each corner of the room.

First there was the one they hope will be the single, "Shyin' Away," written by David Sandler. David co-produced the first Spring album, and has worked on Beach Boys material.

It's a great Top 40 song—the Rovell sisters retain the innocence they purveyed when they were the Honeys, back in the Sixties, and Sandler's melody caters perfectly to their best qualities. I didn't think they wrote songs like that any more.

Then there's David's "Snowflakes" a pretty Christmas song with whispered vocals, and Brian's "Had to Phone You," which he wrote when Marilyn was in Europe and he was still in California. Lastly there's a ballad by Dennis Wilson, one of the prettiest love songs he's written, beautifully sung by Diane.

They all sound like smashes to me, and Brian's production work — reminiscent in many places of his "Pet Sounds" touches, with perfectly-placed oddities like a clarinet solo and a bass line provided by the bottom end of the piano keyboard—is tremendous.

Marilyn explained that they were no longer with United Artists.

"Now how can they drop somebody after only one album? But I'm glad. I mean, they worked hard for us in Europe, but over here . . .!"

Columbia Records are interested in them at the moment, and amazingly they're all like young kids on the brink of their first contract—excited, a bit breathless, wishin' and hopin' like mad. They really want Columbia to like their stuff.

"They were crazy about the first album," said Diane, still stroking Brian's neck with the vibro-massager. "But we're wondering whether they're going to like the new stuff . . . it's so different". Don't worry, girls—the only difference is that it's better.

Brian was still lying on the floor, groaning, and while we discussed Spring I was cajoled by a small beaglish dog called Banana into playing catch with a tennis ball.

It was fun for awhile, but I couldn't help feeling that we were stalling. Time for a prod.

"Oh," I said, feigning nonchalance, "I'm really happy—I've just got hold of a copy of the Students' 'I'm So Young'."

That did the trick. Brian leapt to his feet. Brushed the massager aside, forgot his headache and spoke.

"You did? Oh that's fantastic. 'I'm So Young' by the Students . . . that record took me through senior year in high school. Oh, it's great."

This sudden burst of activity almost overbalanced me. Stand back, speak normal, stand back, speak normal, stand back . . . I only had time to nod in knowing assent before he spoke again.

"Listen here, I think I have that record somewhere . . . I'll go find it."

Finally, Brian reappeared. He hadn't found the record, and he started flipping through a pile of 45s lying on a chair, next to the upright piano.

Then he started putting them on the record-player. First there was "Da Doo Ron Ron," which he played twice. Then "Fool For You" by the Impressions—"That's Curtis Mayfield," he said. I know, I said. He sang and mimed along with the chorus.

He took out an album with "Phil Spector's Christmas Album" hand-written on the blank label, and played "Winter Wonderland," skipping the needle carelessly back to the beginning after the first few bars, over and over again. He seemed to find it hard to drop it at the beginning of the track.

"Does Phil live near here," I queried innocently.

"Oh. . . umm . . . I'm not sure. In Los Angeles . . . or does he live in New York? Maybe he lives with Paul McCartney!" He laughed mischievously, like a little boy. "Where does Paul McCartney live?"

In London, I told him. I think he knew, and it looked like I was getting a put-on, so I asked him about this song called: This Could Be The Night," that he'd told me about before. Spector had apparently recorded it with the Modern Folk Quartet around 1965, and Brian had heard it during the recording, but Phil never released it.

Brian rushed to the piano and demonstrated how it went. He remembered it very clearly, except for a couple of verses. He told me that he was trying to get the lyrics from Phil so that he could record it with Spring, but every time he called Spector seemed strangely reluctant to part with them.

It's a great song, and Brian obviously got a buzz from singing it with differently-harmonised bass lines and new riffs, and it was fascinating to hear how, even though he was only mucking about, the harmonies and rhythms were pure Brian Wilson. No-one else could've been playing that piano.

He also sang the Platter's old "Twilight Time," then sprang up and led me through into a big room which used to be his home recording studio, where many of the finest Beach Boys cuts since 1966 were made. Now it has a bare wooden floor, a grand piano, a few chairs, and many pictures of Marilyn and the kids.

He took me through the room and up some stairs into a smaller chamber which used to be the studio's control room, pointing out where the monitor speakers had been. Newly-laid bricks filled the hole which had been the window between booth and studio.

"Marilyn wanted some more room," he said. "She was tired of having musicians coming in and out of the house . . . but it was a great studio. We got a nice sound here."

He sat down at the piano. It was the very same instrument, Marilyn told me, that had been placed in a sandbox back in the days of "Smile," when Brian had wanted to try and get a certain feeling into his music—the same kind of trip that he went through on the "Fire" section of "Elements," when he got the session musicians to dress up in firemen's uniforms.

Was there still, I asked him, any truth in the recurring rumour that the "Smile" tracks would be released one day? No, he said emphatically. There just wasn't enough left to put together—only fragments, like the snatch of "Surf's Up" around which they re-recorded the song last year. That, then, seems to be it; the final confirmation that the original "Smile," with all its mythical reputation, will never be heard.

But we continued to talk about it for a while, and suddenly Brian hammered out the beginning of "Heroes and Villains" "I've been in this town so long and back in the city I've been taken . . ."

After one verse, he switched into an unfamiliar lyric and tune, and when it was over explained that this was the full original version, as written by himself and Van Dyke Parks. Like several other songs, "Vegetables" for instance, they were hacked around and edited before being released on "Smiley Smile" and 45s. Had "Smile" come to fruition, we'd have heard them in all their glory.

(Later when Diane told Marilyn what Brian had been singing, she said: "No, . . . Not **really**? He hasn't done that in years. That's fantastic!"

Back at the piano, Brian told me about this other song he was working on for Spring. He made me promise not to divulge its identity, but I can say that it's in the "Cottonfields" mould—a Stephen Foster-type song, this time with an arrangement inspired by the Spencer Davis Group's "Gimme Some Loving."

"I gotta get David," he said. "David," he hollered up the stairs. The slight, pale figure of David Sandler appeared, and they sang it together, trying out harmonies and tags—and if it ever comes out, it'll be a classic record.

No wonder Brian didn't want the secret giving away, because anyone who had the formula could do it—and probably botch it up.

Before supper, Diane told Brian to show me round the house. He took me out as far as the gates of the pool, which were locked, and back onto the patio, where kids' toys cluttered the concrete.

He took me upstairs, where the guest rooms were piled with bric-a-brac, and the "master bedroom," where his own bed lurches drunkenly, one leg snapped off. One thing's for sure—the place looks lived-in and comfortable.

By this time, I'd given up standing back and speaking normal. Brian, too, had lost most of his jitteriness.

Next time, I thought, we'll get down to the interview. But meanwhile, it was nice to know that Brian Wilson isn't the madman that legend suggests.

He's just shy, and very nice.

The Giants Rock On

Pink Floyd

by Chris Welch

In their seventh year together, paranoia and fear seem to haunt Pink Floyd's music, despite or perhaps because of success.

Much of the Pink Floyd's recent work reflects the pressures and obsessions that afflict the itinerate rock musician. Without the lifestyle, there would not be music; and without the music, the lifestyle could not be supported.

Mad laughter and sane voices intermingle in the Floyd's measured, timeless compositions, and it would be easy to read into the characters of the men who make up one of the most original and fulfilling of groups, a kind of omniscience.

Fans—and journalists—can and have been disappointed, or surprised to find that the Pink Floyd are but human. Their output is not prolific, they have been known to repeat material at concerts, they have yet to announce details of any plan to save the world, and what is more, they operate and enjoy taking part in a moderately successful football team.

Time wasted, the curse of money, ambitions unfulfilled, these are all matters that concern the Floyd, and form the basis of many of their musical ideas. They are not esoteric subjects and should be easily assimilated without recourse to mystical interpretation.

Yet even today, the Floyd occasionally feel misunderstood. But they can also feel a tremendous satisfaction in the knowledge that the band said to be "finished" when Syd Barrett left them all those years ago, has reached a peak that is impressive even in this age of supergroups.

Acceptance of the Floyd's poised and delicate music has never been greater. On their last American tour they casually sold out massive venues from coast to coast; the "Dark Side Of The Moon" has taken world charts in its stride, while their British concerts sold out as quickly as tickets could be passed over the counter.

The Floyd have doubtless earned an attractive penny in their time, but unlike many other successful artists, they do not wallow in riches.

Roger Waters lives in a modest house in Islington, where his wife bakes pots in the garden shed. And while David Gilmour lives on a farm in the country, it is through his own efforts that the establishment has been made habitable. He might boast an ornamental pool in the garden, stocked with gaily coloured fish, but he dug it himself.

It was to this rural retreat that I drove one sunny day, wending through the fields of Hertfordshire, made fearful by juggernauts wallowing on S-Bends and locals driving dented grey Cortinas at speed.

Arriving at the village at the appointed hour, a further sixty minutes were spent following the conflicting directions of rustics pushing bicycles. Still lost, I consulted a map that seemed to have been drawn up in 1932.

Hurling this aside my gaze perceived a fissure in the hedge opposite. It seemed scarcely possible I was parked outside the Gilmour estate and had passed it innumerable times in the last hour.

Such was the case. In a secluded courtyard an Alsatian stood guard and a venerable old horse clomped about. A youth in faded blue jeans and straggly black hair appeared like Heathcliffe at the cottage door. "Mr. Gilmour's abode?"

"Yes indeed. Come in and have a cup of tea. It will calm you." My motorist's fury began to abate, as I drank in the ornate, but tasteful decor. Low beams, a juke box here,

woodcarvings there—since taking over the abandoned Victorian farm house a couple of years ago, the guitarist had worked hard at improvements.

When he moved in there was no electricity or heating, and he lived rough as he created an open plan living area, constructed a music room, dug the aforementioned pool and cleaned out stables for Vim, his retired brewers' dray horse. He had, even permitted himself the luxury of a swimming pool, following the satisfactory sale of many of the Pink Floyd albums.

Then came Nemesis, not in the shape of a writer to Mailbag, but a man from the council, only minutes before my arrival. He had presented

a copy of the council's plans to build a housing estate on the surrounding greenbelt land, and to compulsorily purchase great chunks of the Floydian paradise.

"We'll have to pack our bags and move," he said with hopeless resignation. Out eyes turned to Megalopolis creeping over the horizon, the threatening blocks of Harlow, poised ready to march.

We toyed with ideas to build a wall of fire around the premises, to be touched off at an instant the bulldozers arrived, and I suggested sowing landmines in Vim's meadow. Eventually we decided it would be more cheering to speak of the Pink Floyd.

For the benefit of new reader George Loaf (12), it should be explained that the group was born in 1967 during the heady days of flower power and UFO. Mr Gilmour replaced the legendary Syd Barrett on guitar, who had written such chart hits as "See Emily Play".

The Floyd went through a bleak period when they were written off but quietly drew about them an army of fans, and went about their creative work, wholly unmoved by the shifting fortunes and fashions that affect their contemporaries.

They are a proud, pioneering and somewhat detached group who sometimes look upon the cavortings of some of their fellow groups with faint dismay, not out of sour grapes, but from purely aesthetic considerations.

But first, what had the Floyd been doing these last few months, and how long had it taken them to conceive "The Dark Side Of The Moon", which I believed was their best yet?

"We did the American tour," said Dave. "We only ever do three week tours now, but that one was 18 dates in 21 days, which is quite hard. We started recording the LP in May last year, and finished it around January. We didn't work at it all the time of course. We hadn't had a holiday in three years and we were determined to take one. On the whole, the album has a good concept. . . ."

Isn't it their best yet?

"I guess so. A lot of the material had already been performed when we recorded it, and usually we go into the studio and write and record at the same time. We started writing the basic idea ages ago, and it changed quite a lot. It was pretty rough to begin with. The songs are about being in rock and roll, and apply to being what we are on the road. Roger wrote 'Money' from the heart."

Money seemed to be a touchy subject for musicians and fans alike. Were the Floyd cynics?

"Oh no—not really. I just think that money's the biggest single pressure on people. Even if you've got it, you have the pressure of not knowing whether you should have it, and you don't know the rights and wrongs of your situation.

"It can be a moral problem, but remember the Pink Floyd were broke for a pretty long time. We were in debt when I joined and nine months afterwards I remember when we gave ourselves £30 a week, and for the first time we were earning more than the roadies."

For a band that relies on creating moods, good sound was essential for the embryo Floyd.

"We hardly had any equipment of our own. We had a light show, but we had to scrap it for two years. We've had lights again for the last couple of years, but in the meantime we developed the basic idea of the Asimuth co-ordinator.

"We did a concert at the Festival Hall with the new sound system, and none of us had any idea what we were doing. I remember sitting on the stage for two hours feeling totally embarrassed. But we developed the ideas, and it was purely down to setting moods and creating an atmosphere."

To digress, what did Dave think of Hawkwind, the newest prophets of the UFO tradition?

"I don't ever listen to them, but they seem to be having jolly good fun," said Dave without the trace of a smile.

What about the Moody Blues?

"I'm not too keen on the Moody Blues. I don't know why—I think it's all that talking that gets my goat. It's a bit like poets' corner."

Dave did not want to be drawn on the subject of rivalry, but he did admit to hearing with pleasure that an expensive piece of equipment belonging to another group had collapsed. The group had recently tried to poach the Floyd's road crew.

Looking back over his six years or so with the group, what milestones did he see in their development.

"There haven't been any particular milestones. It's all gone rather smoothly. We've always felt like we have led some sort of a cult here, but in America it's been slow but sure. This year in the States it's been tremendous, but I can't say why—specifically. We have been able to sell out ten to fifteen thousand seaters every night on the tour—quite suddenly.

"We have always done well in Los Angeles or New York but this was in places we had never been to before. Suddenly the LP was number one there and they have always been in the forties and fifties before.

"No—success doesn't make much difference to us, it doesn't make any difference to our output, or general attitudes. There are four attitudes in the band that are quite different. But we all want to push forward and there are all sorts of things we'd like to do.

"For Roger Waters it is more important to do things that say something. Richard Wright is more into putting out good music and I'm in the middle with Nick. I want to do it all, but sometimes I think Roger can feel the musical content is less important and can slide around it.

"Roger and Nick tend to make

the tapes of effects like the heartbeat on the LP. At concerts we have quad tapes and four track tape machines so we can mix the sound and pan it around. The heartbeat alludes to the human condition and sets the mood for the music which describes the emotions experienced during a lifetime. Amidst the chaos—there is beauty and hope for mankind.

"It's amazing . . . at the final mixing stage we thought it was obvious what the album was about, but still a lot of people, including the engineers and the roadies, when we asked them, didn't know what the LP was about. They just couldn't say —and I was really surprised. They didn't see it was about the pressures

that can drive a young chap mad.

"I really don't know if our things get through, but you have to carry on hoping. Our music is about neuroses, but that doesn't mean that we are neurotic. We are able to see it, and discuss it. 'The Dark Side Of The Moon' itself is an allusion to the moon and lunacy. The dark side is generally related to what goes on inside people's heads—the subconscious and the unknown."

Did the Floyd argue among themselves much?

"A fair bit I suppose, but not too traumatic. We're bound to argue because we are all very different. I'm sure our public image is of 100 per cent spaced out drug addicts, out of our minds on acid. People do get strange ideas about us. In San Francisco we had a deputation from the Gay Liberation Front: 'I hear you guys are into Gay Lib'; I don't know how they could tell . . ."

As a guitarist Dave had been somewhat overshadowed by the Floyd's

strong corporate image. But his virile, cutting lines are one of their hallmarks and a vital human element. Did he ever fancy working out on a solo album, of forming a rock trio?

"I get all sorts of urges but really nothing strong. Put it down to excessive laziness. No I don't do sessions, I don't get asked. Any frustrations I might have about just banging out some rock and roll are inevitable, but are not a destructive element to our band. I have a lot of scope in Pink Floyd to let things out. There are specially designated places where I can do that."

In the past the Floyd have been subject to criticism, not the least appearing in the MM. How do they react to that?

"React? Violently! People tend to say we play the same old stuff—that we do the same numbers for years. We don't. We are playing all new numbers now, except for 'Set The Controls For The Heart Of The Sun'. The Who are still playing 'My Generation', and nobody complains about that.

"We can take criticism when it's valid. But we are only human and we can only do so much. Sometimes it surprises me when we play really well, and spend some time on presenting a special show, like we did at Radio City in New York, and we get knocked.

"Some people dislike the basic premise of what we are all about. Then their criticism is a waste of time. For someone to criticise you who understands you, and can say where you have fallen down—that's valid.

"There are some people who come to our shows with no real interest in what we are doing, don't like the group, so they don't like the concert. We put all the bad reviews into a little blue book."

This time Dave was smiling. (Geo. Loaf, please note. Musician's joke: Gilmour does not really have a "little blue book". He was speaking lightly, in fun.)

As a key member of a band with its gaze fixed firmly on the future, it seemed unlikely Dave would want to reminisce, yet he was happy enough to recall their origins.

"Nick Mason has got a date sheet ten yards long with all the gigs in red ink—every one since 1967. It's quite extraordinary when you look at the gigs we got through—four or five a week.

"We couldn't do that now, not when you think of the equipment we carry. The roadies have to be there by eight in the morning to start setting up. It's a very complicated business. Things still go wrong, but we virtually carry a whole recording studio around with us, all the time.

"In 1967 no one realised that sound could get better. There was just noise, and that's how rock and roll was. As soon as you educate people to something better, then they want it better—permanently. PA's were terrible in those days—but we've got an amazing one now.

"Before we do a gig, we have a four page rider in our contract with a whole stack of things that have to be got together by the promoter. We have to send people round two weeks beforehand to make sure they've got it right, otherwise they don't take any notice.

"There have to be two power systems, for the lights and PA. Otherwise the lighting will cause a buzz through the speakers. Usually a stage has to be built—to the right size. We've got eleven tons of equipment, and on our last American tour it had to be carried in an articulated truck.

"Oh yes, it's the death of rock and roll. Big bands are coming back.

"There was a long period of time when I was not really sure what I was around to do, and played sort of back-up guitar. Following someone like Syd Barrett into the band was a strange experience. At first I felt I had to change a lot and it was a paranoid experience. After all, Syd was a living legend, and I had started off playing basic rock music—Beach Boys, Bo Diddley, and "The Midnight Hour". I wasn't in any groups worth talking about, although I had a three-piece with Ricky Wills who's now with Peter Frampton's Camel.

"I knew Syd from Cambridge since I was 15, and my old band supported the Floyd on gigs. I knew them all well. They asked me if I wanted to join when Syd left, and not being completely mad, I said yes, and joined in Christmas '68.

"I later did the two solo albums with Syd. God, what an experience. God knows what he was doing. Various people have tried to see him and get him together, and found it beyond their capabilities.

"I remember when the band was recording 'See Emily Play'. Syd rang me up and asked me along to the studio. When I got there—he gave me a complete blank.

"He is one of the great rock and roll tragedies. He is one of the most talented people and could have given a fantastic amount. He really could write songs and if he had stayed right, could have beaten Ray Davies at his own game.

"It took a long time for me to feel part of the band after Syd left. It was such a strange band, and very difficult for me to know what we were doing. People were very down on us after Syd left. Everyone thought Syd was all the group had, and dismissed us.

"They were hard times. Even our management Blackhill believed in Syd more than the band. It really didn't start coming back until 'Saucerful Of Secrets' and the first Hyde Park free concert. The big kick was to play for our audiences at Middle Earth. I remember one terrible night when Syd came and stood in front of the stage. He stared at me all night long. Horrible!

"The free concerts were really a gas. The first one had 5,000 people and the second had 150,000. But the first was more fun. We tried to do two more singles around this time, but they didn't mean a thing. They're now on the 'Relics' album."

Where lay the future for Floyd?

"God knows. I'm not a prophet. We have lots of good ideas. It's a matter of trying to fulfil them. It's dangerous to talk about ideas, or you get it thrown at you when you don't do it. We have vague ideas for a much more theatrical thing, a very immobile thing we'd put on in one place.

"Also we want to buy a workshop and rehearsal place in London. We've been trying to get one for some time.

"No we don't want our own label—but we do have our own football team! We beat Quiver nine-one recently, and now there's talk of a music industries' cup. Oh—and we played the North London Marxists. What a violent bunch. I bit my tongue—and had to have stitches."

Opposite:
Pink
Floyd's
Dave
Gilmour

Led Zeppelin (see page 39)

The Giants Rock On

Emerson, Lake and Palmer

by Chris Welch

"Let's talk about gardening", said Keith Emerson, parking his crash helmet and perusing a menu. We were sitting in a coffee shop off London's Park Lane.

Outside in the street, resting against the kerb stood Keith's black 750 cc Norton Dominator, a powerful machine that had just whisked us through the streets of Mayfair.

It was interview time again for the keyboard giant of Emerson, Lake & Palmer, the man who pioneered the Moog synthesiser in rock, who first extensively fused classical orchestras with groups, who is as happy playing

Bach on a church organ, as he is to perform nightly with one of the most flamboyant and powerful groups ever to emerge in Britain.

But Keith was tired and hungry, with a fuzz of beard adorning his face. And he has been interviewed on the subject of ELP and Keith Emerson from Hampstead to Tokyo.

"Now about this group of yours", I began—something along those lines. "What shall we talk about?" countered Keith. "Motor-cycles, now they're very interesting. Or gardening, shall we talk about gardening?"

It seemed sensible to let Keith eat and repair the ravages of an all-night rehearsal. He was due for another one in a few hours anyway.

Later—Keith began to unwind, and seemed disposed to challenge some of the rumours that have been circulating about ELP.

The gossip says that ELP are breaking up, that their last tour was a fiasco, and there was a general malaise within the band. Keith seemed cheerfully unaware of such talk, and instead revealed that they were in no danger of splitting, the last tour had been one of experiment, not all of which worked, and that the malaise was a genuine case of running low on ideas after keeping up a frantic pace for three years.

ELP have always had something "in the bag", a new album, a new tour, some new surprises. For the first time since the cannons roared their salute at their Isle of Wight debut in 1970, ELP have found themselves in a creative trough.

It worries them. But they are certain to do something about it. And they have a lot more music to get out of their system yet. The day we met, ELP had just changed over—via their own label Manticore—from Island distribution to WEA. And their London lawyer, Stewart Young, had just flown to New York on urgent ELP business. It seemed a good point to take stock of the ELP situation.

Keith talked frankly, with due consideration of his various points, and a deal of mirth, as befits a seasoned trouper, as much aware as anybody of the perils and upsets of the rock business.

"We've got a lot of tricks up our sleeve for the next album, and it's a question of what to put where. It's difficult for me to explain them yet. One title for the album has been 'Whip Some Skull On Me"—but there's nothing definite at all. No— I've not been relaxing by any means. But when I was living in London I found it increasingly difficult to write, because of the limitations of living in a flat. It's hard to write at odd hours—if you get inspired at 2 a.m. and you want to play the piano, you get complaints from the neighbours. So I'm really pleased to be out of town. I've moved down to Sussex and I discover we are near neighbours of Roger Daltrey—who is a really nice guy.

"I have tried to write things on tour, but there are so many distractions. Once you step off the 'plane, somebody wants you to be somewhere, there's a sound check to do, or an interview, or a photo session. Then you do the gig, and spend the rest of the night unwinding.

"I did manage to write the Five Bridges Suite on the road. I got inspired flying up to Newcastle, by the noise of the engines. So I wrote the first five bars on the back of an airsick bag. I found it the other day— I think I'll have it framed".

"Yes, the band has gone through a lull in creativity. I don't know what it's down to. Maybe the working conditions have not been right. I know that since I went to Sussex I've found more things coming out of me. I just hope that the ideas will start to speed up now, because we get bored when new ideas aren't coming through.

"We tried out two new things in Germany, and I've always felt that was a bad idea, especially in Germany, just to try out numbers on the road. We've got to believe in them, and the audience still went for the numbers they knew.

"But if you recall the Trilogy LP, when they were new numbers on the show—they got a lukewarm reception. When you saw us in that big hall in Switzerland, the success of new material played in a place like that depends on whether everybody can hear.

"All bands go through this kind of lull. I was surprised to read Rod Stewart's very bold remarks about the Faces position. We've never been in the position before, where we haven't got something scheduled. In the past we've always had something ready in the bag. When we did the 'Pictures' LP, which was live, we already had 'Trilogy' recorded and ready. Now the recording gap has caught up with us. But we just don't want to be rushed into putting something out when we're not happy with it. Sure—there are pressures on us to put something out. It's a funny business we're in. It's a bitchy business, and it's a rat race really.

The thing to do, is not to panic.

"We are all getting more individual in our writing. Greg has written a few numbers on his own, and I've written a few on my own. When we get together it doesn't seem as easy to write as it did on the first LP. It seems to be far easier to write by ourselves. The thing is, whatever we each come up with, it will be used. We have kept up a hectic pace for the last three years and I can feel it slow down. But we are still rehearsing, and I've been writing things for my own LP as well as the band. When things come out of this band it won't be in a big flurry, we'll pace it out a bit.

"We used a lot of experiments on the last European tour—some of which worked, and some didn't. The portable proscenium arch was an experiment, and there was getting Greg to play electric guitar".

Did the controversial arch work?

"No", said Keith quickly, "but we wanted to give it a try. We made the mistake of making it a big star billing, and we were like giving it all this publicity. It was nothing like it was made out to be, and the whole thing escalated, as if it was a bit new production. But all it was, was a new stage and curtains. Many people were very disappointed because they expected God to appear with us on stage and do a triple somersault. The arch was a good idea because at big concerts I have often had to tune up the Moogs in the wings, then move everything on stage, with the risk of pulling leads out. With the curtains, we could set up ready, and waiting.

"We had a grand team of road managers, but they were always late in getting it set up. No—it didn't fall over. But one night a lamp fell off the arch and smashed down on the spot where Carl normally sets up his drums. He had just decided to move them back that night. It was a great shock for him, and quite rightly refused to go on until a safety net was provided to catch anything else that might fall off. There were quite a few safety regulations that were not followed because the roadies were tired, and things got neglected. Yes—the arch was expensive. I don't think we made

much profit on the tour".

Wasn't the tendency for ELP to delve more and more into extravagance, a kind of substitute for new musical ideas?

"No, it wasn't a substitute. The arch enabled us to perform numbers which we would otherwise have great difficulty doing, without the help of a front curtain. We could never have done 'Bolero' for example, and haven't except once in Detroit where Carl had to wear headphones. You see on the album, the number has fifteen Moog tracks overdubbed, and until they develop a polyphonic Moog I can't do that alone on stage. It was a very heavy recording to try and do live, and we tried it before with pre-recorded tapes, triggered off with a foot switch for Carl, who listened to the backing on his headphones. But he got bored doing that and the tapes jammed so that technique was out of . the question.

"The other way was to get Greg to play keyboards, and we brought in another Mini-Moog, which he played with me behind the curtains. Then we opened the curtains and we're all together—doing it. People liked the opening—but after that, nothing happened. As far as the proscenium arch is concerned, we know we failed on that. But we know how to do it now, and if ever we use it again, we'll have learnt by our mistakes. You can only learn by trying things out, by actually doing it. All our roadies have made a date to go to a health farm.

"Morale among the roadies was high at first, but you could see it visibly drop as the weeks went by. When we got to Sweden they all had vitamin shots from a doctor. All fifty of them baring their arses.

"I got this thing that anybody who wanted to, could join us along the road, just to get a trip around Europe. We never did have a roll-call, and I think a few fell by the wayside. I think we left a few roadies wandering around in dressing rooms. 'Excuse me—did anybody see which way ELP went?' Who knows what we will do next? We might all go out and play washing machines on stage". Keith laughed. The comedy of the situation had not entirely

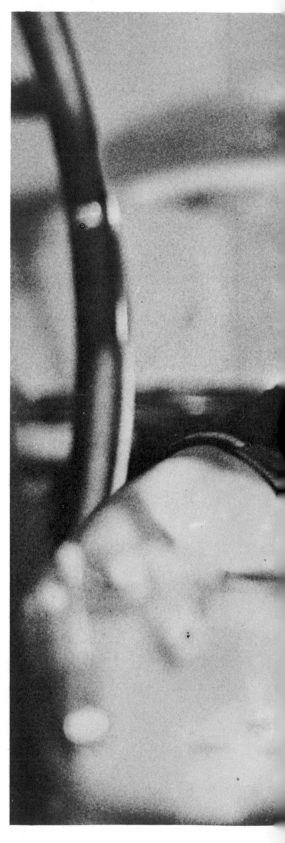

escaped him.

"We had this title for the next LP", said Keith, warming to his theme. "It was called 'Get Me A Ladder'—and this will show how you can slip up. We hadn't even got the first tune down for the LP, but somehow it all got out of hand. It was a pretty far out title and Carl never did like it—and he will thank me for stating that—but he reluctantly went along with it. Then we got sick of it after a week. Next we go on a tour of Europe, and we get out of the plane at Dortmund —and they had three ladders, waiting for us. And they expected us to pose with them. We all groaned, and threw up. Oh no! But we had to live with that—all over Europe. 'Why is your next LP called 'Get Me A Ladder'. And all the group would say to each other—'go on, it was your idea' ".

As a result, Keith is now naturally loathe to be too specific about future plans by ELP, but he revealed he is sussing out a new instrument, to be brought over from America. "I firmly believe it will be good for myself and the band", said Keith. "But I don't want to say too much about it. My ears are permanently open all the time for new things. People think we're relying on new inventions. We're not. We just want to make the biggest sound possible with three people".

"I usually write from the piano. I can write something that sounds good to me, and I'm over the moon for a week. That's not difficult. The hard part is getting it to sound right played by three people".

Has Keith gone as far as he can, with the Moog synthesiser?

"Oh no. Bob Moog is working on something new right now. It's still developing. As I say, it's okay to play something on a piano, but then you've got to get it across to 10,000 people at a concert. We can work as a piano, bass and drums trio in the studio, but the piano just gets lost in a concert. There are no clubs where we can play any more—that's the vicious circle. You are almost governed to write for big audiences. Economics are another factor. To get all our equipment rolling, you've got to keep it rolling. If you stop on the road, you've got to find some-where to put it all. And it's not that we don't use it all. It's not all there for show. So none of it is extrava-gance for which we have been criticised".

Has the fire gone out of ELP?

"Oh no, the fire hasn't gone out of the band at all. The rumours? Oh yeah sure—I know about them. But I believe the band has a future. We have problems, like any other band, but we talk them over, and everything is kept open, so it doesn't explode. That's really the important thing, and we all work well with each other".

"One of Carl's wishes was to have a drum solo on a new number. He played the old one on a number we won't mention".

" 'Rondo'," I mentioned.

"Hmmm, yes. I thought about it for days, and I couldn't come up with anything. Then I remembered a Ginistera piece that was very percussive and I sang it over the 'phone to Carl. He said—'that's good'. And then I played it over the 'phone, and he said—'that's great!' We worked out an arrangement and that was another problem solved".

Did Keith ever worry about the kind of criticism a top band like ELP will run into from time to time?

"I rarely read music papers, but it gets like a bug. You can't ignore them. It's good to know people are criticising us. I really appreciate that. I once saw an excellent criticism of Miles Davis. The guy wrote that Miles was doing this, or maybe he was doing that, or perhaps he's doing it because of something else. He really broke everything down. It was like poetry to read. Actually, there's nothing you can criticise about music. It just goes into the air and it's gone. I think if you read something good about yourself, it does as much harm as if you read something bad. You start to think— hey I must be fantastic. Look this guy says I am. You have to try and ignore criticism, good or bad. If you believe the good things you can end up an ego-maniac".

"I once dug out all the worst reviews of ELP I could find for the programme notes of our last British tour. When people go on show what do they normally get? All that bullshit about how good the group are. So I thought we'd give them a programme containing all the worst knocks we've had, all the downers, and real personal attacks. I remember there was one review that accused me of wearing a codpiece and tights on stage. It was a pair of jeans actu-ally . . ." Keith rolled his eyes to heaven.

"At the theatre, we all waited for the audience reaction to these programmes. But nothing—nobody seemed to take in the notice. We peered through the curtains and there was everybody reading the programmes as if there was nothing unusual about them. So maybe bad reviews don't hurt after all. There must be a moral there somewhere.

"Another time we tried a street survey, asking members of the public what they thought of ELP. 'Is it jam?' one person asked. Or we'd get: 'They're all right, but I prefer Marc Bolan'. The classic one was: 'Aren't they the geezers who had some pictures in an exhibition'. They were all genuine quotes and we were going to use them in an advert. I added a line to say that Island records were flogging off a few LPs and were sending Dave, Chuck and Jeff out on the road, just to show that the record company were on a really personal level with us".

"We had this thing in the States where people come up to you— 'Hello Carl! I've got some great drum books I'd like you see!' And they're talking to me".

After all the years on the road, performing an act that has been noted for its extrovert character, first with the Nice and now with ELP—was the strain beginning to tell?

"I really feel a lot happier on tour, I really do".

But is the wrestling with organs, the leaping and knife throwing, still a real part of Keith?

"Oh yes, it's part of me. I get a lot of urges to do other things now, like flying and motor cycles, and speed in general. It's all part of my weird make-up I suppose. Any-thing fast. I have to get it out of my system. Lots of musicians have been accused of having little gimmicks, but what I do on stage has always been a part of me. The problem is, something that starts off naturally, impresses people. But then it gets known, as a gimmick. Oh yeah, he's the guy that jumps over his organ. But I don't feel compelled to do anything. I do feel annoyed if people expect me to do something that is so obviously a small element of our show, and that it's the only thing they remember. Oh God, didn't the people hear anything, didn't they hear that three part piano figure. Didn't they hear that piece of Art Tatum?" Keith laughed, self-mocking. "Maybe I expect too much of an audience. But as far as that visual thing goes, I don't feel I have to do it because the audience are there to see me do it. I expect they're saying: 'Oh no, he's going to jump on the organ again' ".

"If people expect me to do something, then I won't do it. If I'm excited—then I'll *still* do it. That's why in Zurich I jumped off the stage into the audience. I didn't care where I landed, it could have been a bottomless pit for all I cared. What I do on stage has to be sincere. It can't be phoney". And I knew that Keith was deadly serious.

ELP has been likened to a juggernaut. Did he feel in control of the situation?

"Yes, I do. I have to be, or I couldn't work any other way. We constantly question ourselves. I went back to a music teacher recently, and Carl is going to the Guildhall school of music. I learnt quite a bit, and Carl is getting more lessons in percussion. We're always changing and learning. Maybe next year— we'll all be playing Japanese knee trumpets. Oh, oh, I shouldn't have said that!

"You can say that we will be going back to America this year, and Australia, and I know we should play England, obviously. I'd like to play England when we've come up with new things. We used that European tour as an experiment really, some of it worked and some didn't. It's a funny thing to do really— 'use Europe for an experiment'. Why did we climb Mount Everest? Because it was there. Maybe we'll do other things that don't work out. But we'll have a go anyway!"

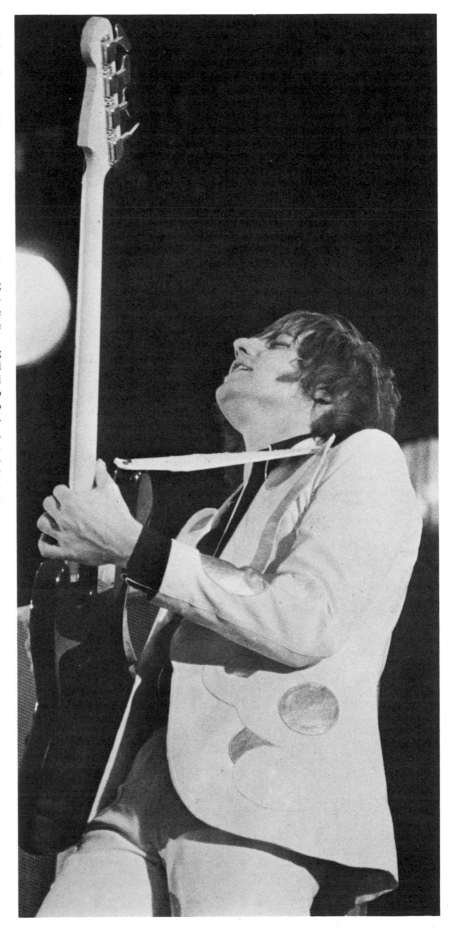

The Black Revolution
Stevie

Wonder

by Chris Welch

Stevie Wonder's new album, "Talking Book", struck me as one of the better releases of 1973. It has those qualities that draw Man to music, as opposed to other sundry diversions.

There is a spark of creativity, and that irresistible sound of talent releasing pent up energy. Yet there are those who claim "Talking Book" is not a patch on "Where I'm Coming From", or "Music Of My Mind". Others yearn for the Wonder of yesteryear, a harp playing Motown child star.

With regard to appreciation of his latest work, I was fortunate in not having been over exposed to his past triumphs. I come with fresh ears to Wonder. And as far as I'm concerned, "Talking Book" says it all.

And as far as Stevie Wonder is concerned, his music says it all. His way of conducting an interview is to ask: "Have you heard this?" and produce a sophisticated cassette tape machine. Music bubbles forth, and you know right away what he's talking about.

As Stevie yawned and stretched and fellow journalists queued in the corridor outside his London hotel room, as I had done an hour before, the question loomed large; was all this babble really necessary?

He had been in London last week, for a guest TV spot, and courteously agreed to stay over for interviews. But it meant a rota system of press and radio men, cramming all discussion in a kind of marathon Talk-In at the Royal Garden.

Not that Stevie was undisposed to talk. With his hat firmly planted over his ears, tinted glasses in position, hands seeking the warmth of a cup of tea, he chuckled drily, groaned in mock despair and occasionally bellowed in the manner of a New York radio deejay. Mostly he answered questions, with due consideration.

One of the songs on his LP is "Big Brother" which to people who have read and been frightened by George Orwell's 1984, is a title with powerful meaning. For some reason, I was surprised to find that Stevie had read the book, and yes indeed the song was inspired, at least in part, by Orwell's vision of a police state controlled by "telescreens" that watch the public, instead of vice-versa.

"I saw the play on TV and read the book about six years ago, as a kid. I don't know if his prediction will ever happen, and it didn't really frighten me. It's kinda hard to be frightened by that, anymore than you would be, by War Of The Worlds. I guess the song is about watching a certain kind of person, black people in the ghettos, people who don't have too much; and about force against force."

The sting in some of his lyrics seemed to come out at unexpected moments on the album. . . .

"Hah—the boy is getting kinda MILITANT! You get back to 'Fingertips' now!" Stevie laughed. "You see, 'Talking Book' is a combination of things that were left over from 'Music Of My Mind' and some new songs. The newest were 'Superstition', and 'Big Brother'. People seem to have changed in their attitude towards me as a musician, and well yeah, it does faze me.

"But I don't feel I've got to get down and do the same kinda stuff forever, I've had chances before to change, and blown them. You have to be cool to new ideas, and today I am able to work more than ever. I always have a lot of tunes in my head that I put together, and work ideas around them. I'm always a year ahead of what's on the last album. But however people compare the latest album to 'Music Of My Mind', this one felt good to me and it felt right.

"Basically . . . I never worry about what other people think and say about me. I want to play a track for you—one song I just put down myself. . . ."

And Steve slipped on the tape machine resting on his lap. After we heard the tune—an inconclusive, but funky piece of music—Steve said: "Motown basically didn't understand what I wanted to do at first. They said—why don't you do THIS? And a lot of people said: 'Stevie—you should stick to your OWN kind of style'. People said I was getting into rock and that I should come on back home. I said—what are you talking about? We as a people, are not interested in 'baby, baby' songs anymore. There's more to life than that! I think singles are very important, but they are only one page in the book. An album is a book.

"I know some of the rock artists don't want to do singles. I don't put aside what I've done in the past. It's just that I don't want to do it anymore. At the same time, you shouldn't allow yourself to become too self-indulgent."

How did Stevie relate to his success, when young? "It didn't faze me. I was very happy and excited. In fact, I couldn't believe it. When I was a kid, I'd sing and everyone seemed to like it. But at that age, I was more interested in candy, and I didn't want to know about Cadillacs. I still don't want to know either.

"I had the experience of going up the chart, and down again, and when people don't want to know you. That way, you don't get no big head! And there's the time when people who you think are buddies, don't come round anymore."

How did he think Michael Jackson would cope with his brand of teenage success?

"Kids are more cool nowadays. They have much more control over their situation. Mind you, I didn't want to have much say, when I was 15."

Did Stevie enjoy material success?

"I don't think so. As far as luxuries go, I like a Mercedes, and the only reason I like it, is 'cos it rides well. Actually, I'd like a palace. I get tired of hotel rooms."

One of the pleasant surprises on "Talking Book" was the presence of Jeff Beck on one of the tracks, and Steve enjoys working with British musicians, particularly Eric Clapton.

"I've spent more time with Eric than most other people—just as people. I remember when we went to see Roland Kirk together." Steve smiled and rocked back on the sofa. "Old Roland really started to come down heavy on English musicians. . . .

"I cut around four to five tracks with Eric, and I hope some of them will be on the next LP. For me, this is like only the beginning of my career and there's all sorts of things I want to do. There's more freedom to do what you believe. But in the South, it seems like people don't come out to see me, and in those big halls, well it really sounds bad when they're empty."

Did Steve manage to recreate his album sound, live on stage?

"I like to get a more spontaneous thing going. We've got some horns, and I'll play the drums on the first tune, but I'm not looking for the same sound we get on the album. To me, the audience is more important. My name is in the studios, but the excitement comes when we put it across to an audience.

"Black music is changing. It's not supposed to stay in one area. You hear people say—soul music is dead. That's what they say (adopts deejay voice that brooks no argument) . . . soul music is dead. But there's no such thing as soul music. If it's a riff, and you're black, when you're a 'soul singer'."

Stevie seemed on the verge of falling asleep as his voice tailed off and fingers caressed the digits of his tape recorder.

"He does that all the time," said Coco, his pretty lady friend, peeping around the bedroom door. "Thanks a lot," said a suddenly alert Steve.

How long had he been doing interviews?

"All day," he responded simply. One of the tape controls responded to a firm poke, and music flooded forth, bringing light into Stevie's darkness.

On his American album covers, he has the title, "Talking Book", printed on the sleeve in Braille, the writing of the blind. Some British copies have also been produced in this way, and Steve was presented with one. He ran his fingers over the cover, and seemed puzzled. "Why did they do that?" he asked. "It says 'Picture Book'!"

The Black Revolution
Sly Stone

by Michael Watts

Can this be Sly Stone, the "black Bob Dylan", of legendary hip, cruel manner, the stoned-out, unintelligible victim whose struggles can be heard to piercing effect on "There's A Riot Goin' On"? Can it be?

Can this be the man, this black dude, draped politely across the bed, answering questions with civility and genuine humour, saying "pardon" a couple of times when he thinks he's misheard, asking courteously for a glass of iced water, cracking jokes with sure-fire disc-jockey laughter—in fact, acting as naturally and normally as you could wish for?

It can. It is. Don't be afraid, gentle interviewer, to venture forth into the lion's den. The sharp teeth have not been pulled, but the mood is benign and sane.

Sly is "up". Not "up, up and away", but his feet are once more on the ground and the mental and physical processes are functioning together to a degree that was doubtful before. Look for the tell-tale, debilitating effects and you'll find none. There's a line on a track from his new album called "In Time" that says it all: "Switched from Coke to Pep, and I'm a connoisseur."

"Sly has realised he's got to get back to realities," says his press agent, Al, a white, Italianate-looking man. "He knows now he's got to live up to the expectations of his fans."

No more late arrivals at gigs, no egomania—working consistently again?

"Yeah, oh yeah." Sly answers earnestly, like a kid, short, snappy and intense.

Tours lined up?

"Yeah, yeah, oh yeah. As soon as they start I'll do a paradiddle across the kitchen. England, anywhere in the world . . . in June, they'll start in June. We'll have a month of rehearsal, a woodshed rehearsal, and then we're gonna go kick ass."

He gleefully rolls the expression around his mouth and lets it out, slow and lascivious. Then he bares those big teeth in the wide mouth and his laughter rumbles deep and jarring: a train passing over a tunnel.

It's the voice that impresses first; subterranean he-man in conversation, it's a remarkable organ which on records never sounds the same twice; a low rumble varying to gull-scream falsetto and then the physical presence.

Body beanpole slight, but muscled and wiry, and the ever-grinning face surmounted by a huge, black aureole of hair, like Marsha Hunt used to affect.

The endless legs are encased in black and red leather pants and the shirt is open to the waist. It's a hot day in New York, and this bedroom on Central Park West is made claustrophobic by heavy, wooden shutters over the windows.

In person there's something of the clever, wilful child, a feeling of spirited malice that he gets away with because his humorous patter is inventive and engaging.

He likes games, likes to test those people who are brought before him with notebooks in their pockets and cassettes cocked.

During an interview with an Italian journalist some time ago he spent the entire time on his knees, cleaning up some dog doody off the floor to the utter distraction of the interviewer.

He's a put-on artist, of course—a special dispensation that seems to have been conferred by higher authority on those whose talent runs deep and who, by virtue of this, can be forgiven. He likes especially word games.

He's a quick mind, twisting sentences and thoughts, and delighting in the aftermath of confusion, then slow recognition, that surrounds his audience.

Ask him about his writing, and he replies, very composedly, "I get more thoughts sitting on the toilet."

Interviewer, considering seriously, "that's the best place to think".

"Well, it's the best place in the world to get rid of waste! And that undoubtedly gives you room to think." (Laughter)

"That's life," someone remarks absently in the room.

Sly seizes on the phrase in an instant, and then he's off, careering impromptu into a kind of dee-jay hipster rap, throwing rhetorical questions at himself:

"What's funny?"
"Life."
"What's Life?"
"A magazine."
"Where'd you get it?"
"Round the corner."
"How much is it?"
"Fifteen cents."
"That's funny."
"What's funny?"
"Life."

Thus does it ever run, a soul package of pop star and disc jockey, which he used to be before the Family Stone was put together in 1966.

Before that, after three years in Vallejo Jr. College studying musical theory and composition, he had produced on the Autumn record label in San Francisco for the Beau Brummels, Bobby Freeman and the Mojo Men.

It's only this year, in New York, that he has begun producing other people again; this time a white, Californian artist, with a light, high voice like that of Labi Siffre, named Jimmy Hall. He is doing it as a favour to the head of Epic A and R, Stephen Paley.

Not that he wouldn't like to produce outside his own music. He mentions, first off, Morgana King, and then Aretha, Ray Charles . . . and Bob Dylan. This, it seems, has been broached with Dylan by Columbia records, and Dylan was interested.

"I'd make him sound the best you've ever heard," Sly says thoughtfully. "I'd give him everything he needed—just depending on the song. I know that I can. I just know that, man." And then he pauses, as if unable to remain serious too long. "Really, I'd like to produce Ted Kennedy. And Muhammad Ali!"

But Ali got beat.

"Yeah, but he shouldn't have. He knows that he shouldn't have. I told him. I hit him in his jaw, that's what weakened it. Thornton, Norton, whatever his name is, he cain't beat Muhammad Ali. Nobody can."

It was you that did it, huh?

"Yeah, it was me." Grin. "You ask him. I'll call him right now. He'll tell you. I faked him out when we were boxing. He wouldn't hit me . . . cause if he did I'd have to hurt him." He breaks out in his long, horse laugh, relishing his remark.

"Oh," he adds, "and I'd like to produce Doris Day."

It was inevitable that somewhere in the conversation her name crops up. On his recent album, "Fresh" ("that's the mood-fresh"), he has a version of the Screen Virgin's old hit, "Que Sera", which he sings almost impossibly straight in his soft, breathy voice; the track seems to go on forever.

He did it because he liked it, but there's little doubt that he appreciates the irony of himself, Super Hip/ Super Stud, coupling with the aforesaid Doris.

He met her through old friend and producer Terry Melcher, Doris Day's son, and over at her house they did the song together at the piano. Contrary to public comment, the duet was not recorded. It was only later he decided to tape the song. But the meeting went fine between them.

"It's not segregated in Hollywood," he leers. "Well, it is . . . but I just never even look at that. I told her, 'siddown, girl.' I showed off; she liked that. Yeah, she's very aware. She's very wise. Only thing, she started talking 'bout the Baptist church and she shouldn't've done that." He snickers loudly.

"Que Sera" was part of the surprise of the album but the real turn of events was the revelation that Sly had rediscovered his appetite for life.

Whereas "Riot" enforced a belief that his private persona was crumbling under the abuse of drugs, self-indulgence and police harassment, this one was untroubled and seemingly unclouded by the doubts and misgivings about his personal outlook, which made certain tracks, like "(You Caught Me) Smilin'" and "Luv'n Haight", rather sombre, if involving, listening.

Some of the introspection of the last album is retained, but it's not confining; there's a drive to the dance floor once more, even if there's nothing quite so unrestrained as "Higher".

It pitches at some place between that period of "Dance To The Music" and "Riot", with the lyrics more refined in relation to the increasing maturity of the writer's experience. A track called "Frisky", for example, whose tempo is precisely that, is followed by "Thankful And Thoughtful", where he sings:

"I've taken my chance, I could be dead.

"I climbed from the bottom right up to the top."

And then, sliding that tongue into his cheek, he includes a sly dog of a song, "Baby's Makin' Baby", that pants in lechery and innuendo.

"It's about grown-ups who are chronologically old enough to handle it," he winks.

"From the womb to the tomb," and that's it, baby, I checked it out.

I ask Sly if he doesn't feel this album is more "up" than the last one.

"That one was down in a way, but it was"—lowers hand in a sort of elevator motion—" 'down' down. Not a down feeling, but down to earth."

According to him, the basis behind this reversal of fortunes was that he was no longer surrounded by incompetent people. "In the past until now there have been other problems that occurred on account of people that were involved," he says darkly and obscurely, before now more things were left in the hands of incompetent people and it naturally affected me."

Like who? Management, tour promoters—what?

He hesitates. "Well, I wouldn't like you to . . . well, anybody around an artist has either got to be a manager, a promoter or an agent. Everything's different now." He leaves it at that.

He believes his reputation for unpredictability is undeserved: that he's been misrepresented by the press. "If they wanted to they could find out what it really was all about." And what it was about was incompetence on the part of others.

But it was often felt he believed it added to his style as a performer if he kept the audience waiting, say.

"Yeah, that's what I mean. A lotta times when they were waiting so was I. I was waiting to go on and they were maybe dickering over prices. I remember one time at a festival, it was cold, man, it was really cold—and that was in Florida —and when I came they kicked all the other groups out the dressing-room.

"They were in my dressing room— cats were in there sleepin', you know what I mean—and they said, 'Sly's comin' get out! get out.' So how's it look? I had to try and collect as many guys as I could and say,' hey, man, come on inside, it's cold. Commonsense. The truth prevails, and for that very reason I don't worry."

At this point he looks totally serious, and I mention all the busts he has had in the past two years— several for cocaine possession, the silliest occurring in early December before a concert at Madison Square gardens when he was arrested by New York police at the Harvey Radio Co. off Fifth Avenue for allegedly threatening people with an imitation gun.

"If you gotta pistol you gotta pull it out," he grins, "especially when its a cap pistol."

So why did they take it so seriously (an old lady called the police when she saw him).

"Because I look serious!" Pause. "No, I had a cowboy outfit on, and I guess in New York, with a cowboy outfit on . . ." He shrugs.

"But if a child should get a cowboy outfit for Christmas with some guns and should go into a store, he could pull it off. So what? What's the age limit? And I still wear my cowboy pistols when I wear my cowboy boots, 'cos I'm a cowboy!"

This expression of "so there!" is writ large across his face. In fact he wrote "Space Cowboy" about his predilection for cowboy wear. "They should've busted me last year for that," he adds mildly.

I asked him what cumulative effect the busts have had on him. "Inconvenient," says Paley, the A and R man, who's in the room. Sly doesn't reply. Okay, so why did they keep picking on him?

"Well, I don't blame 'em," he answers with mock seriousness.

But that period was over for good?

"Well, it should be, it may as well be, because it's all ridiculous. I die for that which I live for, and wearing cap guns is something that I don't believe to be harmful.

"That very day I had spent about 5,000 dollars at Harvey Radio, and the people at Harvey Radio wanted to talk to the policemen and say, 'hey, man, what are you doin? he ain't doin' nuthin' '. But they said, stay out of it or we'll take you down, too. I was just, y' know, practisin' my fast draw. As soon as the white cats start winnin' all the fights with the Indians then it'll be the black guys start doin' somethin'."

By now, the conversation, which has been taped by Sly on two cassette machines is breaking up. His flittering attention is wavering.

There's a pretty blue-eyed blonde there; he whispers something deeply into her ear and she gets up and leaves the room for something. He stands and searches in the wardrobe for new clothes to wear.

Whilst he's thus engaged, I tell him I'd expected to find him very messed-up. He must've had the worst press agents in the world.

"Yeah, I know what you mean," he grins widely. "Just write for me, man, 'cause people have got the right person but the wrong impression, and they don't deserve that."

So who's the real Sly Stone?

"The person who I think you realise." The grin stretches.

That's a cute answer.

"I come up with 'em. I'm funny man!" he explodes.

"Write it down."

And then, buttoning his shirt, the photographer clicking away, his face bursts like an obscene sunflower into that wicked leer. "I'm not fu . . . ed, man," he gasps in mock-pain. Then his eyes roll up into his head and he falls headlong on the bed, as if a half-dozen Quaaludes have just got to him. We all go along with the fun.

Till the next time.

The Black Revolution

Bob Marley

by Richard Williams

Bob Marley, slightly-built and quiet to the point of diffidence, is a leader. He's the master of Reggae, the man who's giving it that big shove out of its normal cultural confinement and into the rest of the world.

The consequences of this action may be drastic for the health of the music. It could be the making of Reggae, or could sap its vitality beyond repair. But that won't affect Marley, because for the past seven years he's been making the best music to be heard in Jamaica, and his potential is limitless.

He and his group, the Wailers, released an album called "Catch A Fire" in March on Island's Blue Mountain label. It seems to me that this may be the most important Reggae record ever made — it's equivalent of Sly's "Dance To The Music," or Marvin Gaye's "What's Going On."

It has that kind of potential: re-vitalising the style from which it springs, and introducing it to an entirely new audience. A few years will need to have passed before we'll know for sure, but Marley may even be a genius.

Like many great musicians, he's a different man inside the recording studio. The shyness is stripped away, and he becomes totally as one with the music, controlling it and swaying in sympathy with the extraordinary rhythm patterns he draws from his bassist, Aston "Family Man" Barrett, and his drummer, Family Man's brother Carlton.

Marley's musical assurance comes from a considerable depth of experience. At 28, he's been burned and hassled as badly as most of his Jamaican contemporaries, but unlike a lot of them he's putting the know-ledge he's gained to good use.

He can see why and how he got burned, and he's going to make sure it doesn't happen again. What's happened to him already, though, gives him just as much right to sing the blues as Robert Johnson ever had.

He was born in Kingston, Jamaica, the son of a white British Army cap-tain from Liverpool — "I only remember seeing him twice, when I was small" and a black Jamaican who wrote spirituals and sang in the local Apostolic Church.

Unlike most half-castes, who violently take one side or another, it's given him an unusually open view of race: "I don't really check people's colour," he says.

Bob sang in church, too, but he didn't care for it.

"I preferred dancing music. I listened to Ricky Nelson, Elvis, Fats Domino . . . that kind of thing was popular with Jamaican kids in the Fifties. The only English speaking radio station we heard was from Miami, but we got a lot of Latin stations, mostly from Cuba, before and after Castro."

He began to learn welding as a trade.

"But I loved to sing, so I thought I might as well take the chance. Welding was too hard! So I went down to Leslie Kong at Beverley's Records in '64, and made a record on a single-track machine. Jimmy Cliff took me there—he was Beverley's number one man."

The record was called "One Cup Of Coffee," and the world ignored it. But Marley, undaunted, went back to the woodshed.

"My greatest influence at the time was the Drifters—"Magic Moment," "Please Stay," those things. So I figured I should get a group together."

He assembled four other kids: Peter Mackintosh (vocals, piano, organ, guitar) and Bunny Living-tone (vocals, congas, congos), who're still with him today, plus a boy named Junior and a girl, Beverley Kelso.

He wrote a song called "Simmer Down." They rehearsed it, and went to see producer Coxon Dodd, who liked and recorded it, putting it out on his Coxsone label.

"It went off like a bullet," says Bob.

"But they didn't tell me how much it sold . . . that's supposed to be the private business of the producer. I don't remember how much I was paid for 'Simmer Down,' because when they give you money, they don't tell you what it's for.

"After we left Coxon in '69, we got no more royalties—and the songs we did for him are selling ever since. We made 30 or 40 records for him, and most of them sold good."

Among them was the brilliant "Put It On," a shimmering Ska classic which surfaced in Britain on Island in 1966, and the gorgeous "Sunday Morning" (on a par with the best of Curtis Mayfield), the B-side to "Love Won't Be Mine" in the same year. If you look hard, you can probably still find them on the second-hand stalls—and if you do, you'll be congratulating yourself for ever.

"We weren't making enough money to share between five, so two of the group left. Junior went to live

in America, and Beverley . . . well, she was kinda slow-like. She didn't have good timing."

After they left Coxon Dodd, Bob and his mother left Jamaica for a while.

"It was hard in Kingston, so we went to live in America, in Wilming-ton, Delaware. I rehearsed by myself in our basement, where it was nice and quiet, but after a few months I went back to Jamaica, and I thought I might as well continue with the Wailers."

He got Peter and Bunny back together, and they decided to form their own record label.

"That's a big move, in Jamaica. Prince Buster was the first to start the revolution by leaving the pro-ducers and doing it himself. Then myself, then Lee Perry . . . and you can't count the rest.

"It's better to know for yourself if your record is a flop, than have some-one else tell you. And if your record sells good, the producer pretends he's gone to Nassau when you come by the office. In Jamaica, you're expected to use your knife, or your machete, or your gun."

That first label was called Wailin' Soul, but it got off to a bad start when Bunny was jailed for almost a year on a ganja rap—and those who've seen The Harder They Come may understand the Machiavellian implications of frame-up behind that.

At that point around '68, American singer Johnny Nash and his manager, Danny Simms, came on the scene. They were looking for talent, saw Bob singing on Jamaican TV, and signed him up.

Bob recorded an album for their JAD label, but from it only one single—"Bend Down Low"—ever saw the light of day, in the States. However they took Bob's song "Stir It Up," recorded already by the Wailers on Coxsone, and turned it into a worldwide smash for Nash, who also used other Marley songs ("Guava Jelly," for instance) on his "I Can See Clearly Now" album.

They even took Marley to Sweden for three months, to help write the music for a film starring Nash which has yet to be released, and over in England they got a single by him out on CBS—"Reggae On Broadway," with which he's far from satisfied because Nash had too much influence on the production.

"He's a hard worker, but he didn't know my music. I don't want to put him down, but Reggae isn't really his bag.

"We knew of Johnny Nash in

Jamaica before he arrived, but we didn't love him that much. We appreciated him singing the kind of music he does—he was the first US artist to do Reggae—but he isn't really our idol. That's Otis or James Brown or Pickett, the people who work it more hard.''

Going to Sweden did Bob's business no good: "When I came back, it was all mash (ruined). I'm the only one who takes a real interest in it. Jamaica's a place where you sit around and get high. I'm not gonna do that: I get high, but I don't like sitting around too much."

So on his return, in 1970, he started a new label, Tuff Gong, and also a record shop. The Soul Shack on King Street in Kingston. The shop is mostly devoted to selling records by the Wailers and Rita and. the Soulettes. Rita Marley is known as Bob's wife, but they aren't actually married—it was just an idea to get some publicity for one of her records.

They stock the old Wailers records on Coxsone, their six 45s on Wailin' Soul, and the dozen-or-so they've released on Tuff Gong, including their biggest hit to date—the fantastic "Trenchtown Rock," which sold about 25,000 and was Jamaica's number one for three weeks around Christmas 1971, and the recent mind-destroying "Satisfy My Soul (Jah Jah).''

The problem for a small label is getting airplay: "You have to be big friends with the radio disc-jockeys, take them out and treat them like family. They make up the radio station charts, and people only buy what's in the charts.''

Bob is not unduly optimistic about the business side of the Jamaican music scene.

"We've hurt the big guys by starting our own labels, because all they've got left is the studios and the pressing-plants. But the business will only change when younger guys appear, who'll deal fairly with the artists. The older guys will never get better."

It was Island's Chris Blackwell who gave Bob the chance to use a lot of time and a fair amount of money to make the "Catch A Fire" album. Advances to Jamaican artists are unknown—but Blackwell saw the potential in Marley, and the two men tacitly decided to trust each other.

The result is the first example of Marley's music which hasn't been hampered by absurdly low budgets.

The album has several quite long tracks, maybe the first extended Reggae songs, but Bob says: "They're always like that in the studio, and then they get cut down to three minutes or something.

"Jamaica is a place where the musicians are restricted, going into the studio and just playing the same old thing because they're afraid that anything different might not sell.

"What we need here is people who're not concerned with holding the artists down. But I don't think it'll happen for a long time.''

Make no mistake — Marley is potentially a giant figure.

Below: Bob Marley and The Wailers

73

Gamble and Huff

by Michael Watts

*Leon Huff (top)
and Kenny Gamble*

It's being said around the music business that Philadelphia will soon be back on the map. It couldn't happen to a more depressing city.

Philadelphia is dull, washed out with that sort of mediocrity which makes it instantly seem like the American equivalent of Birmingham. Perhaps it suffers from a sense of impoverishment by being so close to New York, which is only slightly over an hour away by Metro train, just as Brum nurses its inferiority complex from its proximity to London.

Philadelphia shares certain problems with New York. It has an extremely large black community—

some put the ratio as high as 60:40 in favour of blacks—and street crime is now pursuing all those who fled out to the suburbs; between 1970 and '71 some studies show that the crime rate rose by 23·4 per cent and drug deaths have increased 37 times in the past five years.

Still, the Mafia there is the most dormant in America. Even the racketeering, you infer, lacks colour.

So quite what it is about Philly that made it such a big music centre in the fifties and early sixties—with the success of the Cameo—Parkway label and Dick Clark's American Bandstand—isn't readily apparent.

True, there's the big black population, but then Washington has an even greater one and that city hasn't attained any musical prominence.

Clark, of course, was instrumental in pushing local talent like Fabian and Frankie Avalon on Bob Marcucci's Chancellor Records, and Chubby Checker on Bernie Lowe's Parkway label, but his show wasn't necessarily Philadelphian in character or spirit as Thank Your Lucky Stars, say, promoted a certain Birmingham flavour (in fact, the programme is still going—televised from the West coast).

The city doesn't breathe any musical life. There are only a few clubs and two main concert venues, the Academy of music and the Spectrum, the latter catering for the majority of the big rock acts who hit Philly; there is no sense of anything new and indigenous happening within the city itself.

The success of Philadelphia in the old days of Cameo-Parkway and Chancellor (together with Swan, who released Freddy Cannon's records) seems to have been predicated less on the quality of the music—which was, after all, riddled with gimmicky dance crazes like The Twist, and popularised by good-looking but vapid white boys such as Bobby Rydell and Fabian—than the sharp opportunism of businessmen and the circumstances of American Bandstand being networked from there.

Philly just happened to be the right place at the right time.

It's the factor of big business, I think, which has pushed the song-writing and production team of Gamble and Huff to the fore after a decade of working out of Philly and its environs.

Two years ago they signed distribution rights of their label, Philadelphia International to Columbia, the largest and most prestigious company in the States, and they did so at a time when Columbia was anxious to get a secure foothold in the black R and B market.

Columbia responded by putting to work the reputedly best distribution department in the American record industry.

Accordingly, in the past year or so Gamble and Huff have had almost simultaneous production hits through out the world with the O'Jays "Back Stabbers", Harold Melvin and The Blue Notes' "If You Don't Know Me By Now," Bill Paul's "Me and Mrs Jones," and many others. It was in their studio, too, that the recent million-sellers

by the Stylistics and Spinners were recorded.

The impetus of good promotion and the right sort of exposure has made all the difference, because it's not as if the two men have only just started making good records.

From 1967 to 1969 they produced a string of hits for Jerry Butler on Mercury—such stuff as "Brand New Me," and "Never Give You Up"—and Wilson Pickett's first Gamble-Huff single for Atlantic, "Don't Let The Green Grass Fool You," became his first gold record. It's a question of breaks.

A former label, Neptune, started in '69, and distributed through the GRT corporation, featured good records by the O'Jays and the Vibrations, but it all fell to pieces the following year after Leonard Chess, their essential contact with GRT, died.

This time there's been a change because their own names have been inextricably linked to the success

The O'Jays

of the records which have made it, and thus, too, is it being said that Philadelphia is once more undergoing a musical resurgence.

As if in confirmation of this fact, Barbra Streisand is expected to record there shortly, and that will authenticate, too, Gamble, Huff and Sigma Sound Studios out of which they work.

Sigma Sound itself looks nothing particularly special. It has a modest front on 212 N 12th Street, a few doors away from the Central Gospel Hall.

There are two studios, but one has only just been completed and the equipment including an automatic mixer, has still to be fully installed. The main studio is really small, about the size of a modest living-room, and one would imagine it's incredibly cramped when strings and horns are on a session.

There's a battered upright piano, and just underneath the control glass, covered by canvas, the set of vibes

belonging to Vince Montana, a white sessionman who invariably works on the Gamble and Huff recordings.

The engineer on these sessions is Joe Tarsia, a dapper, bird-like man in his mid-thirties with grey, Perry Como-style hair and a neat pullover. He's seen all the comings and going in Philly.

"Bernie Lowe?" he raises a quizzical eyebrow. "He's at home counting his money. But he's a nervous man, always did have problems with his nerves. He's been in and out of hospital."

You ask him if there was a lull in recording when Dick Clark pulled off Philadelphia, and he says sure, but it didn't last for long, and on the walls you see the gold discs for the Stylistics, the Intruders, Delfonics and others.

The studio hasn't suffered. And right now it's expanding. This month Gamble and Huff are moving into the old Cameo-Parkway· building just across the road at 250 South Broad Street, and Joe will be in charge of the two studios on the third floor.

You can see the former home of Chubby Checker, the Orlons, the Dovells and Bobby Rydell—all those names from the early sixties, if you look out the front windows of the Gamble and Huff offices. They're on the sixth floor of a building which houses the local Shubert Theatre on its ground floor level.

Gazing out, across the slick of rush-hour traffic, you notice that the third-floor windows of the Cameo-Parkway building are eyeless in their yellow canvas blinds. It's low-slung and rust-bricked with a worn air to it.

Next door they're erecting a huge condiminium, a pompously newfangled name for a block of service flats. It's beautifully poetic justice that Gamble and Huff, who did a little work for Cameo in its heyday, should be installing themselves in this old stamping ground.

Gamble and Huff's present headquarters are too low-keyed to seem prosperous. The building is old, and the various offices are a little dog-eared. Even the masters' quarters, though well-furnished and carpeted, are subdued and a little gloomy.

On one wall is a green board, on which are chalked "future" and "present" sessions. The Futures top the former category, somewhat appropriately.

Earl Sheldon, Vice-President of

the Gamble and Huff concern, which currently consists of Philadelphia International and Gamble Records, shows me round. He's young and black, as are the half-dozen executives involved in the company (they employ three white office girls).

Sheldon, too, has his Cameo-Parkway links. He began there as an errand boy ten years ago and worked his way to head of A and R. Now he drives a purring maroon Buick.

I'm not sure if he's being self-deprecatory but driving back in the car from Sigma Sound he says that he once taught Music Ed. but he knows nothing about the music side of the Gamble Huff. He starts laughing.

"Before 'Backstabbers' was released, Kenny asked me if it was gonna be a hit and I told him 'No, I don't think so.' Now if I say something's bad, it's bound to be a success."

Kenny Gamble, now 29, comes from South Philly. In his teens he was a medical technician, with hopes of becoming a doctor, but he tinkered around with guitar and piano, and at the age of 18 wrote "Everybody Monkey", which Freddy Cannon recorded.

He then became a songwriter and arranger for his own group, Kenny Gamble and the Romeos, which featured himself on vocals, two brothers, Roland and Karl Chambers, on guitar and bass respectively, Earl Young (ex-Stevie Wonder) on drums, and Thom Bell as the keyboard man.

Together this group made four or five records, none of them successful, but they've stuck together as a nucleus for sessions, adding a few others, like Norman Harris, a Wes Montgomeryish guitarist, and organist Len Pakula, as the years have gone on. By general consent it's this rhythm section that has made Gamble-Huff so distinctive.

Out of the Romeos, in fact, has come a figure whose renown is as great as that of Gamble and Huff. Thom Bell, a slim, stylish 30-year-old, is now a business extension of Gamble-Huff enterprises, with his own record label coming through shortly.

Bell has cut a reputation for himself as a superlative arranger—he did the charts for "Back Stabbers" and the Blue Notes "I Miss You"—and has been particularly associated as a producer with the Delfonics and, more recently, the Stylistics. But back in the days of the Romeos,

he was replaced on piano by Huff.

Leon Huff comes from Camden in S. Jersey (he now lives near Philly in the palatial Cherry Hill area, where Muhammed Ali has a house). He's 30, and has knocked about a little more than Gamble.

For two years he worked with Quincy Jones in New York. He played on some Phil Spector dates with the Ronettes, including "Baby, I Love You" and on Coasters' records.

He was with Leiber and Stoller and Jeff Barry and Ellie Greenwich. Carole King he worked with when she was married to Goffin. And before he met Gamble he had a national hit, "Mixed Up, Shook Up Girl", with a hometown group, Patti and the Emblems.

Eventually though, he moved to Philadelphia, where he worked with a number of local bands, including a

Harold Melvin

female group called the Three Degrees (whom Gamble-Huff are currently producing). These rehearsed in the same building as Kenny Gamble. That's how they met.

Their first song as a team was "Together" by the Intruders, who shortly gave them their first gold hit, "Cowboys To Girls," in 1967. Now they own two record labels and three publishing companies: Assorted Music, Downstairs Music and World War III Music.

Their personalities are quite different. Gamble sits behind his desk, serious and cool, explaining the progress of their careers as if if it were some business transaction. He looks impassive behind his rimmed glasses, but he still does virtually all the talking. He's the businessman ("my business is my world, and that's all I can go by").

Huff says little; he wears a vague disinterested expression that seems to mean he'd rather be some place else, in the studio most likely, rather

than talking about how they made records. But then he's the more musically active of the two. It's him you hear on piano on all those records. He plays a lot of drums too.

"A regular one-man band," says Gamble, mildly sardonic. Huff sniffs.

But it is still a team. Huff generally works on the rhythms while Gamble basically does most of the mixing. That's the most specific difference, but there's no set pattern.

"We get together every step of the way," Gamble remarks.

There's a good story about Huff in the studio, though. On one of their production sessions for the Laura Nyro album, "It's Gonna Take A Miracle," Huff spent the entire time on the telephone, except during the breaks, when he went and sat in on piano and jammed with the rest of the musicians. Then a girl came in and off he walked with her.

But essentially they have a format in producing, Gamble explains.

"We get all our ideas in the office before we go into the studio. Everything is put on tape before it's recorded so we can listen to it back with just piano and voices—the main thing is the performance of the artist and whether the song is really right for him or not.

"Then we go in with chord charts. Me and Huff record different from Tommy Bell. Tommy does all the arrangements but we create the tracks in the studio. That's why our rhythm tracks have a lot more goin' on with 'em because we do 'em strictly from the head.

"Rhythm that's the strongest asset we have because basically the rhythm is all our arrangements.

"We do the rhythm first, and then we overdub voices, and then put on strings, and horns and whatever, duplicating most of the patterns of the rhythm. We try to let the rhythm emphasise certain parts of the tune."

For Streisand (if they can settle on some dates) they intend to cut an album from which a bunch of hit singles can be pulled out.

"We'll cut hits, which she doesn't have now, and consequently she'll sell twice as many albums. We'll design material especially for her, create another sound for her, utilising her voice and vocal ability."

The idea of recording her originated with Clive Davis, former head of Columbia Records, which is also Streisand's label. Gamble agrees that their deal with Columbia was a turning-point.

They'd figured if they couldn't make it with that company they

"For a whole year there was a mix-up because they'd never been involved in black product before on a constant flow."

Now Gamble Records is being distributed through Columbia along with Philadelphia International, and they're repackaging a lot of old Neptune product—albums by the O'Jays and Billy Paul—for re-release on Philadelphia International.

Then, of course, there's new product, like Roland Chambers' group, Yellow Sunshine, the Three Degrees, a girl act called the Mellow Moods, and the Futures, "who're gonna be fantastic." Plus Gamble is seriously thinking of cutting his wife Dee Dee Sharp of "Mashed Potato Time" fame.

Trying to account for their success, Gamble points to an overall change in the system of exposing black music. They feel able now to cut singles with the concept of an album in mind because albums of black music now have a vehicle to be heard with the increasingly powerful black FM stations.

The big record-selling stores are also being made aware of the change.

"The big stores have started buying black faces to put on their racks. You know, there used to be a time when a black artist couldn't put his face on an album if he got a hit record. It was questionable; it would hinder the sales of his album. So you just put the buy's name there and a picture of a pretty girl to disguise his identity. I've been in situations like that where that kind of a situation is going down."

It upset him?

He shrugs.

"Nah, it don't matter to me. If that's how fickle it is, that's the way it is, you understand."

"But it hurt a lotta people who were becoming big stars," cuts in Huff.

The situation, however, has now been reached, reflects Gamble, where a black artist doesn't have to depend on a white public to sustain him and can therefore become popular with his own people without having to go through any "whitening" process.

And with the volume of the black market increasing, this leads to better communication between the two cultures, inasmuch as a lot of pop songs that have never been exposed on black stations can now become successful in negro communities via black artists.

"It don't really matter to us, this race thing," adds Gamble.

It's not inaccurate to say, though,

couldn't make it with anybody. But the success of the venture didn't happen overnight.

that they'd like to build up a kind of Motown complex in Philadelphia. Berry Gordy, they mention, has always been the man who gave them the idea they could really make it.

"That's basically our whole thing," says Gamble, "to establish as many black people in the industry as possible, 'cos we are black—there's no getting away from it.

"I think our sound is maybe a continuation of a Motown sound. It's basically just good soul music that appeals to both black and white.

"Most of our records start off black and have to achieve a certain status on black stations before they cross to pop, and there are a lot of our records that are never heard on the pop scene which are big on the black stations. So I would imagine

Billy Paul

black people buy our product most because it is originally black."

They have no clear definition of their sound, although they feel there is a certain indelible Philadelphian influence in there, citing gospel singers, for example, like Clara Ward, who got their start at the Met in Philly.

And then they point out that the city IS predominantly black, an emigre population derived from Alabama and the North Carolinas, for the most part.

If they had begun recording in earnest in New York, say, the result would have been different:

Huff: "Kenny and I thought New York was too much of a hassle. There's so many of 'em, record companies all over the place. We felt Philadelphia was more settled, more relaxed, and it wasn't too much of a hustle-bustle type of thing. Plus there wasn't that much competition down here."

Gamble: "It's the vibrations that really count, it's the feeling. It's

like if you go and sleep at somebody else's house the feeling is different, you don't feel like you're at home.

"It's really making a place your home, and you feel like you can make mistakes there and do whatever you want. If you go to another studio there's people watching you, that type of thing, and it's not the same atmosphere. The atmosphere in Philadelphia makes the whole thing connect.

"We've drawn attention back to Philadelphia again. It's rejuvenating the whole city, and a lotta people are coming here now. Once you start to get hyping a lotta talent, it comes.

"That's what the city needs—a lotta talented people. Most of the talented people went to Motown for a period.

"But I remember when a lot of 'em couldn't get into Cameo-Parkway. WE couldn't even really get in there when they were hot. They had their own people in there, Kal (Mann, label executive) and Bernie.

"They had four or five people they were interested in, and I don't think they cared about developing new writers and producers. I don't think they could see too far."

This time around, of course, there's no American Bandstand to pump specifically Philadelphian product across, but Gamble dismisses the show's influence.

"There were no blacks on those shows," says Huff, "except every now and then they'd have a black person on to demonstrate the dances."

So, what price Philadelphia? If Gamble and Huff and Bell do put Philly back on the map, so to speak, at least it will be more for musical reasons than for those of image and gimmick as in the past. But it's doubtful if it matters that much.

A good producer can cut a decent record anywhere—it's what or where feels comfortable to him. All the talk of "music centres" these days seems something of a conceit.

It's not so much happening in Philadelphia, really, as in the heads and hands of three young men. That's what it always comes down to.

It is right that the Lady Sings The Blues movie should have brought its star, Diana Ross, to fresh prominence. Right also that it should restore the recordings of the original Lady to a prominence they have consistently merited.

Lady Ross is delighted on both counts. Proud of her film performance and the nomination it earned, though disappointed at not winning the award since she gave all she could to what was a super-juicy part. And gratified to see Holiday albums being issued in droves.

"You're selling Billie's records as well as your own," I said when she sat down next to me in an ornate room in London's Inn On The Park.

Dressed in a white open-necked shirt, with a double rope of pearls, high-waisted plaid pants and doubtless a few other articles, she looked as sharp and sparkling as a diamond, and much more expensive.

"I'm telling you she's selling a lot of records!" she answered. "All of them are coming out again, and you know what? Here in Europe they

have completely different cover pictures of the ones I have at home. This is something that fascinates me; you've got a whole new set of Lady Day pictures."

She is an inveterate collector of Billieana, who has read everything, looked at or listened to everything, pertaining to Billie that she could lay hands on.

Bits of writing on photographs are scrutinised by her, and she tries to find out the identities of faces included in groups with Billie. Some of the photos have come to her from Billie's personal collection.

These photographs, like the records, played an important part in helping the actor-singer to build up her film portrait. She studied carefully the clothes Billie liked, and how she wore them, and this lent a certain verisimilitude to the portrayal.

"You know the episode where I wore that fur coat and the sun glasses. I took those from pictures, the pictures of her on the train."

Clearly an expert on the Holiday picture gallery, she even has photos

with me in them, and remarked earlier that she recognised me as "the gentleman that knew Billie in England." I was grateful for the description.

Because of all the publicity around the slogan, Diana Ross Is Billie Holiday, it is quite likely to become the fashion to say that she is not and to knock her for, so to speak, trying it on.

However that may be, I find it impossible myself to withold admiration from her loving and in many ways self-revealing representation of a woman who was at once emotionally frail and easily assailable, fiercely independent, aggressive, temperamental, supremely gifted.

My strongest impression each time I see Lady Sings The Blues, is twofold.

One is the filmy artificiality of a story line which leaves out almost all the "highs" of Billie's life except those which were drug-induced. And the other is the transcendent quality of Diana Ross's performance, especially when singing those

The Black Revolution

Diana Ross

by Max Jones

Holiday numbers which come within her reach.

I was curious to know whether the conception of these interpretations—which periodically conjure up visions of Holiday mannerisms and magic—was her own or whether she took much guidance from musical director, Gil Askey.

Well, she said, the first portion was hers. "In other words, during my research, when I spent a lot of time with her music, I made my own decisions. But when starting the film, the musicians helped an awful lot.

"I spent time with some of the gentlemen who knew and worked with her. Sweets Edison was one, and there were quite a few others who had played with her. They helped me."

Diana emphasised that she had not wanted to play up the addiction aspect of her subject, preferring to show a side of Lady she thought young people today would not be familiar with.

Billie was a beautiful and talented performer, and she wanted to make her seem more than "just a drug addict." More than once she pointed out that she hadn't written the film's script.

In my view, which I expressed, the film does not even hint at the years of artistic satisfaction Billie must have enjoyed (in part at least). I said that most of us here, who knew her at all, knew and admitted her as a singer.

"What I'm saying," she came back with a suggestion of impatience, "is I tried very much to show her as the performer that she was—drugs was just a minor part of her life that had happened earlier.

"It was a tragedy that it happened, but the most important thing in her life was her craft, and her love for people and for her music, and showing that, feeling that.

"I speak about her sometimes really as if I met her, and then I say to myself after I leave you and go upstairs: 'How can I talk so factually when I only read these things and only spent time with pictures and her music?'

"I've made this imagination of a lady, a legend, and I had to try to play that part. It's very difficult for me, and every day I find it more difficult, because I ask: 'Am I wrong by feeling that I knew her as well as I feel that I did?'

"And I've come to argue with people, you know, about the facts. I felt that I lived with her for over two years. I talked to many people, and say if there were four people, those four knew a different Billie Holiday.

"From their memories some knew her as a very bitchy so-and-so; some remember her as a sweet, loving, giving person; some as being very vulnerable, open and not able to cope with world problems, or her life or whatever.

"People saw her so differently, and I had to take all of these things and put them together to make the lady that I played on the screen."

One of the striking characteristics of the true Billie was her physical toughness, the very real ability to mix it with men or women on more than equal terms.

Miss Ross is not quite big enough, I remarked, for all that knockabout stuff although she does a very good violent scene with Billy Dee Williams in the movie. "Lady Day really would have knocked him down." I told her.

"I felt that I could, too." She laughed throatily. It was the kind of sight and sound calculated to send less busy men tottering to the bar for moral support. Still, I continued with the line about dissimilarities.

"You don't appear to have much in common with Billie," I said, "because you look as though you've led rather a protected life and are a middle-class lady, whereas the real Lady was brought up rough in the slums of Baltimore and was raped at the age of 12."

"Uh-huh, I know, I have lived a protected life."

Obviously, the traumas of the young Billie created a personality hard to impersonate, though I allowed that in the pre-cut version Diana Ross made a game attempt within the soap-opera context.

She said thank you, and added: "Well, I'm not going to tell you whether I was raped at 12." The impossible lashes stayed down for a moment before they dissolved into laughter.

Later she claimed that knowing Billie, as she feels she does, has altered her life and made her a different woman, a better more honest one.

Is there not a danger, then, in all this identifying with Billie, that she will find it hard to go back to being plain (that is to say, beautiful) Diana Ross?

She said that really she didn't care. "Guess what I've done. I've lived two lives in my lifetime. I mean I really totally, bodily, got involved in this lady's life.

"I would wake up in the morning constantly thinking about what Billie's thoughts may have been in comparison with mine that morning. Or, as I put a gardenia in my hair, if I were she what would the feelings be. That has made me a different person."

Ah, the gardenia. I believe Billie Holiday began wearing one because a handsome admirer gave her a fresh bloom each day. Diana agreed that was a good reason.

"The same thing happened to me in Las Vegas. Someone sent me a nice bouquet of gardenias, and I wore them that night. I hadn't planned to, because I didn't plan to go on the stage as Billie Holiday. I wanted to go on the stage as Diana Ross.

"But I wore them that night, and ended up wearing them most every night because I really loved them and they gave me a feeling of feminity. And they smell really good and the fragrance lasts for a long time."

If that is identifying with Lady Day then Diana Ross was content to own up to it, saying that she liked to identify with something she thinks worth identifying with. Which sounds logical enough.

"But she happened to be an Aries and I'm an Aries. We were both born in April. I don't know if that meant anything, but also the key range she sang in, I happen to sing in that same key range. I had to change none of their keys.

"These maybe are things that don't mean very much, but somehow they begin to mean things to me. She had a nasal quality, and I've always been said to have had that quality in my voice.

"So when I started to learn her music, the many songs I fell in love with, I didn't have to learn them. I mean, it kind of just happened with my body, and then it kind of happened with my head.

"I argue with people about what my feelings are about Billie Holiday. It is amazing really, because I wish that I could have met her just once, or seen her. But then all of a sudden I felt like I had, and that I'd known her for a long while."

At one time it was thought the film might use a genuine Lady Day soundtrack, the leading player miming to Billie's voice.

Such miming seldom if ever convinces, because one artist's facial movements and gestures don't really fit another's, and I sympathise with the decision to let the former Supreme make a complete job of the role.

Diana Ross, at any rate, stated her position firmly. At first it wasn't clear whether she would be required to lipsync Billie Holiday records. She said:

"I thought that would be an insult to her and an insult to me, being a singer and a performer.

"So I decided that, without trying to imitate her in any way—because I knew that I couldn't and that also would be unfair to me, being a singer—that I would just listen to her music and try to learn about jazz and the time when she was performing.

"Because if I knew about her life, and what was happening in the world and everything, I thought it would come out through my music.

"I learnt the songs lyrically, but I didn't put feeling in them until we started doing them for the film. Because it mattered where we were going to place the songs; it mattered whether she was on drugs or off; it mattered whether she was with a happy love life or not."

Another question or two wanted to be answered. The Bessie Smith recording of "Tain't Nobody's Bizness," which young Billie is supposed to have listened to repeatedly, turns into a more innocuous version by a Tamla artist.

Why not use Bessie's version? Well, they have someone else singing Billie's part and, in the same way, somebody's doing Bessie's. A strange sort of logic there. But did Diana Ross know Bessie Smith's work?

And the Ross interpretation of "Gimme A Pigfoot" is not much like Billie's recording. Was Diana familiar with Bessie's recording of that? She nodded and said she had listened to Bessie's albums on many occasions, and also listened to many other artists during this period.

Was Dinah Washington among them, I guessed. A bullseye, and the mobile features expressed enthusiasm.

"See now, I knew Dinah: I met her. She was from Detroit, and you see she had an effect on me too as a personality and artist. Yes, I did listen to Dinah's blues. She sang loads of them.

"I think Billie was a gorgeous, gorgeous girl, and she was happy sometimes and this was what I felt: I wanted to show the happiness in her life.

"But I get angry when all I see is pictures of her with tears in her eyes. It makes me really mad because that's not the way she was."

It would have been pleasure indeed to carry on with such talk in such attractive company. However, other inquisitors awaited.

I promised Diana Ross copies of my rarer photographs so she can continue to live the life of Lady.

*Opposite
and overleaf:
Diana Ross
in the film
Lady Sings The Blues*

David

The Battle for the Boppers

Enough human emotion was expended at the Empire Pool, Wembley, earlier this year, that if such energy were harnessed, it could power a small township for several days.

There was a great wailing, and sobbing; a gush of air expelled from many thousand tiny throats, sufficient to blow a man down.

But the man in question, one David Cassidy, love object of a new generation of concert patrons, stood up to the gale force of adulation, and blew what they used to say in ye olde rock scene parlance "a mean set". Several in fact.

Who and what is this mystery figure who comes among us amidst such hullabaloo and furore? Is he merely the product of the much discussed publicity machine, a talentless buffoon, dangling from the strings of the manipulators? Is he just a piece of smiling, plastic cheesecake?

Not entirely—perhaps, not at all. From the evidence of his tough schedule of concerts—six at one venue, each before 6,000 capacity crowds—he is a professional entertainer, happy in his work, and possessed of a healthy degree of talent.

A rather disappointing verdict for those who came to mock, but Cassidy is a lot better than many a teen idol who has trod the boards of the cavernous Empire Pool before him.

It was in the same echoing edifice six years ago, that a well known popular group performed, largely assisted by backing tapes, who were accorded similar acclaim. There was no such monkey business with Mr C. He won his applause admittedly largely due to the smile that now peers down at the populace from the same anti-litter posters where once Marc Bolan held sway, but at the same time showed he had real vocal ability and an understanding of the art of rock that communicated, even through the screams.

The fans, nearly all girls, all under 15, converged on Wembley in that show of force that instinctively arouses aggressive violence among the more atavistic of the male population.

I arrived on Saturday for the lunchtime show, which started at 12 noon, and there were pressmen who had seen the previous night, genuinely angry at the treatment they claimed had been meted out to some of the more hysterical fans.

Doubtless they are difficult to handle and impossible to communicate with in reasonable fashion. But the sight of dog handlers showed an element of ruthlessness not always evident when football fans go on the rampage or tougher prey take over a rock festival.

Perhaps it was early in the day, but my Cassidy concert was a comparatively orderly affair.

The sun shone brightly and the wheelchairs brought in the handicapped children, the coaches brought up the youth club outings, and mums and dads staked out in the car park.

" 'Ere, do you like David Cassidy then?" A slightly older girl gave me what once might have been called

by

Chris

Welch

Cassidy

an old-fashioned look as I strode in burly fashion through the infant throng.

"Doesn't it make you sick!" said a uniformed attendant of the "more than my jobs worth" school, resting momentarily from his labours at the chocolate and confectionery kiosk. His lady friend clucked sympathetically over the Toblerone. It had doubtless been a deafening few hours for the staff, and there was more to come.

After the brilliance of the sunshine, the inside of the Pool seemed to be in total darkness. An overpowering stench of oranges smote my nostrils, and then came the first shock wave of screams.

Even behind the inner wall of the Pool, it caused a sinking sensation in the stomach like dropping into an air pocket while flying a DC-9 over the Italian Alps.

Fumbling through the gloom, special Cassidy passes were produced to thrust under the noses of the guards around the front of stage.

All speech was impossible, and as MM photographer Barrie Wentzell and self staggered past the barricades and out into no-man's land, the roaring of music and cyclone of screams became a "portable ambiance" that no artistic director could conceive, let alone recreate.

We've all heard of artificial environments and total experiences in sound, whether in an art gallery or funfair. Nothing could compete with 6,000 small children screaming at David Cassidy.

Time was momentarily suspended and all consciousness was directed towards the podgy youth striking postures with his posterior on stage.

Clad all in white, with a sunburst on the now famous bottom, he wriggled, leapt and held out his microphone to sing of love and rock and roll.

There was David—only inches away, smiling, and avoiding the gaze of the camera men, toiling with their shutters.

Having sat in many a dusty orchestra pit, spotting the plastic smile is now but child's play. But it can be said, that this newest of showbiz idols seemed to be genuinely knocked out, and digging the whole affair.

He smiled as if he had just consumed many of the oranges I had detected on my way in, and was bursting with Vitamin C.

He tore about the stage as if it were a tennis court, and even the slightest movement, from eyebrow to ankle, was a signal for further hysterical outbreaks.

Seated at the piano, he played a

most tasteful accompaniment to a belltoned version of "Breaking Up Is Hard To Do." Snatching up a guitar, he played some down home blues that surprised me. Was the other guitarist really playing the lead? No, it was David. managing all but the trickiest bits.

Hurling himself upon a spare drum kit, he whipped up a solo that reminded me of Mickey Rooney in "Strike Up The Band". It wasn't half bad. And when 'ere he gave vent to voice alone, he was in tune, and free of all noxious distortions.

So—how bad? He could do with some more original material. Some of the ballads were a bit dull. And he could improvise a bit more in his stage movements.

But when it came to a driving version of "I'm A Man", and his own "Rock Me Baby" . . . like, the kid had rhythm, y'know that?

After the aforementioned ballad, a chant developed that was oddly low-pitched and formed the phrase "We want David", as if there were any danger of him quitting the stage.

But it was interesting to note that during the quieter numbers, the fans did listen in rational fashion, and there was no need to beg for silence as in the days of Beatlemania (The Beatles, beat group popular around 1963–69).

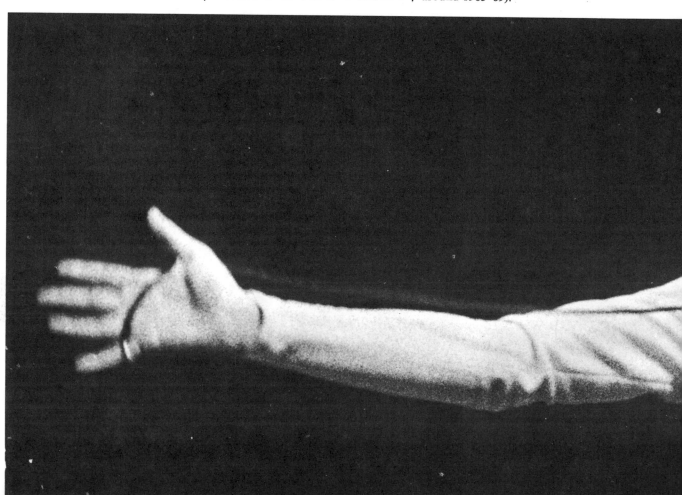

"Here's a tune we've never rehearsed. We just played it in the dressing room, and it's the first time I've sung it on stage. It's one of the three sides on my new maxi-single " . . . SCREAM.

Turning to gaze at the sea of tear-stained faces, biting lower lips and waving arms like tiny tendrils, a lump formed in my throat and a tear filled my eye.

Harmless and happy they seemed. Even the hardened musicians in the backing band seemed to be digging the gig, including, unless my watered eyes deceived, one time MM jazz poll winning saxophonist Vic Ash.

They included tenor, trumpet, trombone, lead guitar and two backing vocalists, Kim and Dave, and the sound they achieved on "I'm A Man" and "Blues Power" was pretty funky. And Cassidy seemed to appreciate their efforts more than the usual front man with backing band set-up.

"How Can I Be Sure" was handled in workmanlike fashion and was greeted with as yet unsurpassed fervour. "This is the first time I've appeared in Britain and you're really fantastic. I appreciate all of you coming—I really do."

After "Rock Me Baby" had stomped its course, there came a strange quirk to Cassidy's day of triumph.

He tore from the stage, hustled through the back door by a waiting aide, doubtless to be whisked by car to the Esso Hotel. But instead of the anticipated howl for encores, there was not a solitary cry of more.

It was as if the audience fully understood the star's need for a hasty retreat and dutifully picked up their banners and oranges, and began to file out as if school assembly was over.

A compere rushed on to shout, "The show's over. David's definitely gone." But this appeal was needless and then it occurred to me that probably a large percentage of the audience had never been to any kind of concert before and were not aware of the obligatory custom of demanding "more". If the man says the show's over—the show is over.

Outside the second house was beginning to build up, accosted by the salesmen of Cassidy memorabilia, and already chanting "Why are we waiting", as they pressed up against the glass doors.

It seemed like a nice gesture if I gave two spare tickets nestling in my wallet for the second show to a couple of luckless fans, who would doubtless be quite overcome at their good fortune and regard me as some kind of magic benefactor.

"Free tickets for David Cassidy," I cried out, waving them in enticing fashion. Blank stares greeted me. Others backed away or scowled. Nobody interested.

Eventually we approached a small knot of fans who looked as if they couldn't afford a ticket and had come along to peer through the fencing.

"Free tickets for David Cassidy. It's all right, they're not forgeries . . ." There were no blank looks this time. Instead, a sour faced girl of some 12 years, snatched them out of my hand, and snarled: "Stoopid!"

Avoiding my gaze, and virtually ignoring my presence she and her friends glared at the tickets as if they were an obscene publication. And instead of the tearstained thank-you's there was a mutter of foul language.

By this time, the lump in my throat had subsided and the choked-up feelings aroused by the spectacle of childish innocence had been replaced by a desire to strangle the next David Cassidy fan who wandered past.

But I hope the ladies enjoyed the show.

The Battle for the Boppers
The Osmonds

"Who are the Osmonds?" asks the middle-aged man with the short socks and shorter hair riding in an airport limousine as the Caesars Palace sign comes into view proudly proclaiming the Osmond Brothers as headliners.

Who are the Osmonds indeed! Ask any 12-year-old who stopped blowing her allowance on clothes for her Barbie Doll and started shelling out shekels for "Top-To-Toe personally autographed with exact measurements" Donny Osmond posters and "Darlin' Donny Kits" with "a huge double, almost life-sized Donny-O poster" and "20-count-'em-20 brand new, never before-seen Donny portraits."

In less than two years the Osmonds sold around 19 million records, earned 12 gold albums and singles, and collected 10 of those within a one year period to beat the year records set by the Beatles (9) and Elvis (8).

Who are the Osmonds? The Osmonds, mister, aren't simply a musical group, they're big big business.

"We better decide on a show and make our reservations early," says short socks to his good grey wife.

You bet, because the Osmonds are doing capacity business at Caesar's 900 plus seat Circus Maximus nightclub. The junior misses in demure gingham granny dresses or nearly waist high minis are elbowing the high rollers out of the choice ringside seats for a better view of Donny.

It wasn't always like that. It took The Osmonds 15 years of hard work starting around their Ogden, Utah, home playing for civic groups at $10 a night. Singing on the streets of Disneyland brought them to the Andy Williams television show and success as a middle of the road act.

Suddenly, not quite three years ago, "One Bad Apple" hit the charts like an A-bomb wiping out their past of middle-aged music and making them superstars in the rock world.

Jay, the 18-year-old drummer, remembers: "The first concert after 'One Bad Apple' was the scariest thing. Before that at the shows we did no one screamed or anything. And after 'One Bad Apple' and 'Sweet and Innocent' we did our first concert in Cleveland. When we walked out on stage, I thought that something went wrong. I was ready to go back off stage. I didn't know what was happening."

"It was mass hysteria," says 24-year-old lead guitarist Alan. "All those flash bulbs. I went blind."

They've gotten used to the constant screaming and flashes, but success hasn't turned their heads at all. Even the sourest cynic would have to admit that the Osmond Brothers are all nice, decent, warm, levelheaded human beings. As devout Mormons, they don't drink, swear or smoke cigarettes let alone go near anything stronger.

When George, 57, and Olive, 49, got married 29 years ago they began having children with a frequency that makes family planners despair. First came Virl, now 28, and then Tom, 26, both deaf and now helping to administer the performing Osmonds' business.

Then came the musicians, Alan, Wayne, 22 (guitar and sax), Merrill, 20 (lead vocals and bass), Jay, and Donny, 15 (keyboard and lead vocals), followed by Marie 14, who is cutting a country and western record and finally little Jimmy, 10, now belting a couple of numbers each show.

Suite 666 belongs to the Osmonds. That's why two pistol packing security guards wait at the elevators to shoo away the camera toting girls popping out of the elevators as fast as dimes are fleeing into the slot machines downstairs.

Inside the huge living room of suite 666 where the pile on the rug sprouts like wheat in Kansas the Osmonds are sweating and panting. They've just finished their first karate lesson given by a guy who could double for Richard Chamberlain and is supposed to be the best black belt in the world according to his famous pupils.

"We're doing this," says Alan, after introducing himself with a warm smile and leaning back on the royal blue semi-circular couch, "because we're very physical anyway and we like the sport. It's something everyone should really know and it keeps you in shape. It's very active. We like things that are very hard and masculine and incorporate that into our dancing."

"It's good to know karate," says Merrill, "In this business you never can tell who is going to come up to you and do something to you."

By this business he means the rough and tumble world of show biz, but spending time in the land of Os, you forget that's what they're in until you see them explode with talent on stage.

I can't quite picture Tom Jones or Mick Jagger behaving like Donny did on our first meeting. Wearing a faded purple tee shirt with "Donny" in white letters across the chest, he says "Hello, I'm Donny," as if you

hadn't seen his face staring at you from the cover of every single teen fanzine. And he's not putting on any act. Conceit just isn't in the Osmonds dictionary.

As if you didn't know already, Donny is beautiful—he could make a dirty old lady out of me. He stands tall and straight like a young Indian brave and his smile and frequent laughs set his liquid brown eyes sparkling.

Even when he's just sitting chatting shyly, you can't miss the star quality that practically glows. Someday he'll be a matinee idol of the kind Hollywood hasn't seen since the young Gary Cooper.

How does he react to seeing his face on all of those magazines?

"When I was young," answers Donny in a strong voice that's changing into a man's, "I remember walking by and just for fun looking at the magazines and it's sort of hard to believe that I'm in that position. All of us are in that position. Sometimes I just can't believe it. It's

really great—and—we owe it all to our fans because they're the ones that make you—really they are."

And he and his brothers mean that. Mr Osmond, a white haired heavy set man always wearing a jacket and tie, interrupts for a moment. "There's a little girl outside who's been standing there for hours and she's baked you a cake. Can she come in for a minute to give it to you?"

Jim Morey, a personable young man who serves as one of their managers, would rather say no because they could be letting girls in 24 hours a day, but Father is a soft touch for the fans and the boys can't resist. Wayne quickly clears away the remains of a cake baked by another fan and Jim opens the door and not one, but at least 15 girls, trip in led by the mini-skirted young baker.

"Girls, no autographs, we're in the middle of an interview. We really broke a rule to let you in," says Jim Morey, but it's in vain because the boys are signing and it's 15 minutes

before Jim ushers the girls out by telling them they better get in line if they want to see the show because people are already starting to go into the Circus Maximus almost two hours before show time.

The boys, much to their dismay, are virtual prisoners in their rooms. The first day there for this their first headlining Vegas gig, Donny snuck out to the tennis courts but Caesars Palace had to ask him not to do it again, because 40 or 50 girls quickly charged.

"I slip out sometimes," says Alan, "but when we're travelling on tours, they lock us up almost. They just say it's for our own safety because we do have kids climbing up the balconies. We had a rope come down the balcony the other day in Florida. It's not that they want to harm us, they just want to get to us so for those reasons we have security guards all the time."

"It's hard to get out on the road," says Jay, "but it's part of the business and we love it. We like to be nice to our fans and of course, they're very loyal. We respect our fans. We know we couldn't be here today unless it was for them."

Not only are the fans loyal but they're persistent and Mrs Osmond says they've had to change their telephone number, listed under a phony name, five times in the past year.

"The operators sometimes give the number out," smiles Donny. "We have two lines and had to change both of them because they somehow found out both. One girl was really sneaky. She told a friend I have to call my mother collect and when the friend got the bill our number shows up." Donny's face broadens into a mischievous grin.

Even at Caesars Palace the night before at the late show about 30 or 40 girls charged onstage and started grabbing the brothers. Donny says that it doesn't frighten him, though it's run through his mind that he could get trampled.

"Nothing has really ever happened dangerously," he says. "I mean, well, there have been a couple of times that we've gotten hurt and like they rush the stage and pull you off. That's dangerous. One time we were trying to get on the bus and some girl grabbed my ear and my hair and the policeman was pushing her away and pushing me on the bus. Then at concerts we have our monitors right in front of us and I went down to shake someone's hand and they pulled me right on the monitors."

Donny adores the screaming he and his brothers induce in the fans, but pauses shyly and chuckles a little nervously when asked to analyse why the girls flip over him. He agrees that perhaps they think of him as a friend and nods: "Well, actually I'm the same age as them so they can relate to someone their own age. I don't really know. That's a hard question."

Though he's been singing since age four, he means it when he says: "I don't think I'm any different than anybody else. We're all human beings but it's taken ten years of hard work and we hope that we can just stay up there and please our fans."

Mrs Osmond, a stout woman with luxuriant jet black hair, recalls that Donny first started singing at age four when he imitated Andy Williams numbers perfectly. "I'll never forget his debut," she says. "The boys were opening for Phyllis Diller at Lake Tahoe and Donny had just learned that old song 'I'm A Ding Dong Daddy From Dumas.' There was a staircase on the stage and he came down the staircase wearing a little tuxedo and top hat singing that song. I wish I had a picture of that."

Donny started out singing with his brothers doing a few numbers as Jimmy is doing now. Then when the boys were in Muscle Shoals to record "One Bad Apple" they each recorded the lead part, but it worked best with Donny.

"That was when I had a high voice," says Donny. "We put it on our album and got a lot of response by mail from kids saying that they'd like it as a single. It was a big decision whether I should sing by myself, whether it would look like I'm breaking up the group, but we finally decided to go with it."

He cut his first solo album when he was 12, but there's no chance he'll go off as a solo artist and there's not a trace of jealousy in the others about Donny's success. MGM's young president Mike Curb, played the original 1958 Paul Anka "Puppy Love" for Donny once.

"It was far out," Donny laughs. "Mike Curb really thought it would be a hit record and he had a lot of confidence in it."

The confidence paid off as both American and English record buyers proved.

The whole Osmond Family except for the two oldest boys travel with the Brothers as well as two managers (Ed Leffler and Jim Morey), two roadies, two sound men, three

agents from Dick Clark Productions, and eight backup musicians called the American Underground. They carry 12 speakers, what Merrill calls "a gigantic sound system," plus assorted odds and ends like Mrs Osmond's sewing machine because she loves to sew.

I attend the Sunday evening early show with Mrs Osmond. On the way down along passages marked "employees only" I tell her how the frenzy of the lobby and casino has boggled my mind.

"You can feel the evil there," she says and then starts to say something about how she hates for the boys . . . but doesn't quite finish the thought.

I'm curious whether what seems to me the sexual response of the small fans bothers her, but she doesn't think they're old enough to know about that. "I think it's very wholesome," she says of the response, "that excitement they have. They're harmless. All little girls grow up with stars in their eyes."

We walk into the tightly packed, tiered Circus Maximus and sit at a booth smack in the centre,

Within seconds a dozen squirming girls, a few no older than little Jimmy, were on top of the table asking Mrs O to sign autographs which she did patiently until the waiter suggested that perhaps she might like a moment of peace. "The show's about to start, girls," she said still writing, "so you better sit down to see it."

George Kirby, the comedian and impressionist, strolled out on stage. "Look at all the nice faces," he said. "You kids are lucky your parents pay for you—night after night after night." He went through the usual impression of old movie stars and even threw in Count Basie playing the piano but the Count could be Queen Elizabeth's cousin for all those kids knew.

Mrs Osmond whispered to me that she liked him because he does no blue material. The Osmonds as headliners decided who would open

for them and they have a clause in their contract against anyone doing any lewd or suggestive material.

Finally the lights went down, the curtain closed and a movie screen descended as the fans screeched with sheer joy.

A film of the Osmonds in concert flickered on the screen as the band played an Osmonds' medley. The screen went up, the curtains parted, more screams filled the air and six dancers in white pants and bare midriff tops writhed out on stage under neon profiles of each boy hanging from the ceiling.

On each side of the stage a silver ramp descended and the boys dashed down and burst into "Down By The Lazy River." They did all those fancy steps and turns singing away while little girls lifted up their napkins and flapped them in the air. Alan introduced each brother but coyly ignored Donny and cries hit the ceiling from the girls.

During his "Go Away Little Girl" and "Sweet and Innocent" solo Donny walked off the stage into the audience and immediately five girls were wriggling next to him for a kiss while thirty or forty others tore up to the front lines. Somehow with the cool grace that only real stars possess Donny managed to jump back on stage to continue with his brothers.

The Osmonds wore white tuxedo jump suits and each boy had a different colour embroidered lapel and stripe down the pants. Donny's colour, of course, was purple—his favourite as any fanzine reader knows. To please the older people as well as their fans in Vegas they mixed in a "Fiddler On The Roof" medley and what they called a living scrapbook of their past working their way through from barbershop medleys up through rock with a stop off in between for all five to play saxophones.

"That's my contribution," said Mrs O beaming as if she'd never seen the show before. "I taught them to play saxophone."

The kids freaked out when little Jimmy, a pudgy tyke sprung out on stage in his tuxedo jump suit with a wide white belt slung low on the hips to launch into "Heartbreak Hotel" and "Hound Dog." No, he'd never seen Elvis, he told me, but he sure got El's motions down pat.

Anyone who scoffs at the group as exponents of "cradle rock" ought to see them do "Shake Your Music Maker" and "Dance To The Music." Sure, they're slick if slickness means you don't stand around on stage in a pair of faded blue jeans tuning up for forty minutes, but they are showmen in the tradition of the great r'n'b acts, dancing up a storm and socking everything they've got into tight harmonies and musical exhilaration.

The next day Wayne reflects: "There's still the excitement of coming here to Las Vegas and head-lining even though we do rock concerts as well. It's very prestigious. Very few people can do both.

"That's one thing we've always enjoyed in our careers and that's the freedom to be versatile, not to do strictly one thing, because we like to cover the whole spectrum of show business."

The next night, I find myself humming "There's No Business Like Show Business" picking my way past empty music stands, coiled wires and busy stagehands backstage at the Circus Maximus room in Caesar's Palace. Donny Osmond, a program book tucked under one arm, is knocking on the door of the Gold-diggers' dressing room.

"I caught you sneaking in to see the girls," I tease him.

He grins and says he just wants to get their autographs for someone. On the dimly lit side of the backstage area not far from a few musicians getting set up for the show, Alan, the oldest singing Osmond, chats with a Golddigger in costume, skin tight black trousers and top that bares much chest and more midriff. Alan could have been looking for replacements for his "big black book" that was destroyed in a hotel fire in Memphis not long ago.

Earlier in the day Donny pointed out that the blaze not only cost the Osmonds a notebook containing songs they had been working on for several years, but also his brothers' little black book of girls' phone numbers. Alan chuckled and said his book was big. Though Donny says he's just getting into dating, the others all make time for girls.

"We like to get out and do the same thing that other guys like to do." Alan told me in the Osmonds' suite. "You can take a girl to the movies in Los Angeles without being mobbed. There's a lot of people walking around that you recognize in that town. It's still difficult. You get approached. They come up to get your autograph. You have to accept it and live as normal a life as you can."

Donny admitted that he still gets butterflies in his stomach before a show.

"You always want to do that extra special job," Donny explained. "We all make mistakes sooner or later but you always want to give a good job for these people who paid to see you. And that's why we have to get up mentally and physically before a show. And that really takes a lot you know."

Aside from vocal warm-ups, getting up even includes a couple of football exercises before the show and after each show I saw, the Osmonds got into a huddle in their changing room to discuss the performance. They've only been at it for 15 years.

"Did you ever think about the past?" Merrill, sitting quietly on the blue couch, asks me.

"What do you mean?" I reply.

"I was just thinking about what I did as a little kid," he says. "We were up at 3 a.m. to milk the cows and do chores and then we went to school and came home and did home-work and practiced our music."

The Osmonds couldn't be more American if Sinclair Lewis had written their story. Back home in Ogden, Utah, they began singing together for church family nights with inspiration from both Mrs Osmond who taught them to play the saxophone and Mr Osmond who used to sing in a high school choir and always sang when driving the car.

Gradually, the brothers achieved a local reputation doing barbershop harmonies and travelled 50 or 60 miles to sing for clubs or organisations at $10 or $15 a night. They worked up to $20 and $30 for Miss Utah pageants and the like.

"We could buy ice cream cones with the money," says Alan, "but it was experience and that's one thing that I think has really helped us now because we have a lot of things to fall back on, a lot of experience and you can't beat experience."

Their grandfather encouraged them to make a film at a local TV

station and they sent it to big net-work television shows but never got any response. Undaunted, the family hopped into the car and drove to Los Angeles in 1960 where they tried to audition for Lawrence Welk but didn't get to see him.

"We had a lot of dis-appointments," remembers Alan, "so we said let's have fun and go over to Disneyland. We were all dressed alike because our mother always made our shirts, each in a different colour. At Disneyland we met a quartet who were singing the kind of music we were singing at the time and they said, hey, you look like a little quartet. We said we are, how did you know!"

So the boys sang a song, a crowd gathered and soon the Osmonds got themselves a job as street singers at Disneyland for the follow-ing summer. They appeared on a local TV show called "Disneyland After Dark" which was seen in a rerun by Andy Williams' father after the Osmonds had returned to Utah.

Meanwhile Mr Osmond had sold his insurance business and so when Andy Williams' father called with an audition offer, they returned to Los Angeles and signed a five year con-tract with Andy. He put them on his own label distributed by Columbia, Barnaby.

"Nothing ever happened," says Alan. "It wasn't the right situation and Andy's been real good to us. He gave us our start but it's been mismanagement in the earlier stages and we were hurt a lot. That's all I want to say about it. It was a growing thing."

Rock and roll was happening and the Osmonds itched to get into it. "We got on Andy Williams show," continues Alan, "and we were doing all these show business things and we were digging the rock scene and we wanted to make a move. We gradually forced more and more of it on to the show and it got to a point where we had to make the decision about going out on our own.

"We talked to Andy about it and told him. He once told us a long time ago, one of these days you're going to leave me like I left my brothers. We said no, Andy, never, never. We left him." Alan pauses and chuckles softly. "It's only natural. It's like when a person gets married or moves away from home, it's a growing period and we took that step."

They had been told they'd never be a record act, but they talked to Mike Curb, president of MGM

Records.

"We said to Mike," Alan recalls, "look, our dream is to eventually have our own label, to record and be recording artists. We've been told that we can't make it, we have faith that we can. He said I have faith you can too. So we signed a couple of years ago just before we did 'One Bad Apple'."

Although the family has a home in Utah where they can really relax, they spend most of their time when not on the road, in Los Angeles where they're building their own studio. Alan says it's going to be the best because they've got it set up with the latest in electronic equipment.

"Donny is really great at engineering," Jay points out." Donny and Wayne basically. They know how everything works and they're going to wire it together."

The boys are excited too because they are producing and writing their own things now. Alan, Wayne and Merrill do the writing with Jay and Donny making contributions. They are trying to find time to write four songs for Donny's next solo album.

Ever since "One Bad Apple" the Osmonds have been haunted with accusations that they've ripped off the Jackson Five. I apologise for bringing that up, but Alan, obviously used to it, reassures me: "Don't be sorry about it. There's nothing to really be upset about. We don't believe in copying."

Jay point out: "When we recorded 'One Bad Apple' we thought Donny had a good voice—how else can a high voice sound."

"Had a good voice," jokes Donny whose voice has lost the high-pitched quality of youth.

"How else could two high people sound but alike?" Jay continues.

"How can brother groups sound except like brother groups?" asks Wayne.

"We've always done choreography so we didn't copy that," Jay adds.

Alan concludes: "If you want to get into it, we were performing a long time, but you can even push that aside if you want. We got down to Muscle Shoals and we all recorded the solo on 'One Bad Apple' and when it comes down to what we think is sellable it turned out to be Donny. Actually Merrill sang the solo whereas Donny just did a few choruses. But then you go by your next record. Was that a copy? And then the next. I would definitely say 'Crazy Horses' is not like the Jackson Five."

They're also used to being put down as teenyboppers or bubblegum and Alan at first says that kind of criticism would bother anyone.

"It bothers them all the way to the bank," manager Jim Morey notes.

Alan laughs and goes on: "All the way to the bank—right! We have fun recording. We wouldn't trade our audience for anything because we have the most loyal fans that I think you could ever have.

"The only thing that hurts is when we have sent a record out to radio stations and they don't tell anybody who it is. They play it and people come in and say, wow, that's heavy, that must be Led Zeppelin or Rod Stewart. When they hear it's the Osmonds they say yeugh, really. That's what isn't fair. Sometimes people have a tendency to put labels on things and the labels get in the way of reality."

"Slick" is another word often applied to the Osmonds but Alan points out: "At one point we were being criticised a little bit for being so-called slick. This was the time when a whole lot of groups just stood up in their jeans and played, but now we maybe have a lead on them because people like Mick Jagger are coming out in a jump suit and getting into light effects.

"People are expecting more of a show. They like to see something different that they can't just see on the street. They want a little effort put into it instead of just sitting there and listening to an album which they could do at home. They want to get the excitement. That basically is what an entertainer provides."

Rock and Roll Women

Yoko Ono

by Michael Watts

There's a touch of irony in the fact that among those sympathetic to the campaign opposing the deportation of John and Yoko from the States was Playboy magazine, one of the major symbols of sexism, which in a recent edition spoke of the "hearteningly broad" range of support for the Lennons in America.

The two of them were doubtless grateful for any encouragement but it was a slightly quirky juxtaposition considering Yoko's strong role as a feminist. But then again, a good pair of boobs have long gone hand in hand (sic) with the magazine's suitably hip liberalism.

The Lennons haven't been seen much of in recent months. John sits cross-legged on his huge bed with the black satin sheets, flicking the channels on the large colour TV that

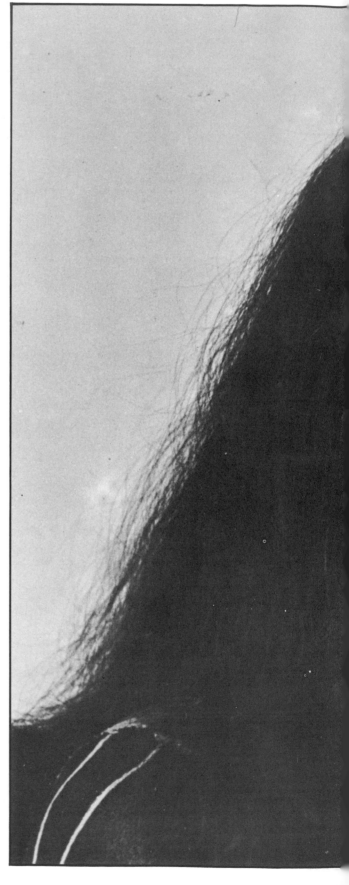

sits at the foot of the bed like a wise Buddha.

And Yoko does whatever she does. Most recently this has been the making of a striking double album called "Approximately Infinite Universe", which was written entirely by her and co-produced with John.

The album is extraordinary for several reasons. Chiefly, it explodes the myth that she's a talentless artist on the make.

She has settled for a more conventional way of creating music than the screams and sighs with which she's been generally, and dismissively, associated, and the enhanced accessibility reveals a gift for poignancy and sensitivity of mood and lyric.

It is painful, but poetically so.

It is also, in many of its lyrics and in an article of hers printed on the album sleeve, a rather sympathetic and certainly un-rabid appeal for a more feminised society—a society, however, which I'm sure would not include Playboy.

As she states in her article, which is an abridged version originally published in the *New York Times*, her aim is for a world that is non-competitive but organic, based on love (feminine), rather than reasoning (masculine).

But she isn't necessarily carrying a banner or strapping on armour. In fact, her song, "What a Bastard The World Is," she wrote as a satire on the militancy of the female Lib. movement.

"So they would scream and shout and kick out all men", she explains.

"Then what are they going to do?"

The Lennons live a rather quiet life these days.

It probably has to be. The threat of eviction from the US Immigration authorities looms large and Yoko still hasn't found her daughter, Kyoko.

There's one word that is always writ large in the conversation of these two. That is "pain".

Although their company is fun and quicksilver, they don't mind admitting that some of the hard knocks get through to them.

There's something somehow embarrassing about hearing this word in an emotional context. It's so very bare and personal. But they apparently have no trouble with it.

Yoko's album was conceived in a state of some pain. This had to do with immigration and her daughter, and then both she and John were depressed about the election and its implications for society.

"Is Winter Here To Stay?" one of the songs, was written after McGovern lost.

But it was, oh, so many things. Being a woman was one, and being Japanese didn't help. It was just the world, really.

"They were pretty hard on me, you know".

She supposes, she says, that before this album she was getting desperately lonely. She was waving a flag for things she believed in, but it was a lonely road in a way.

She got more desperate about communication, which has always been the basis of any project she has been involved in.

"I think all my other things, like the screaming and moaning and sighing, do express certain emotions just as painful as this one, but just because of their abstract nature . . ." The sentence trails away.

"Probably words are more tangible, more acceptable".

She's sad that the public still thinks of her essentially as Mrs. Lennon—ex-Beatle John's wife in England—rather than what she does and has done as an artist.

She's in her 40th year now and her artistic status is relatively unknown; or at least, relatively unappreciated. She's a celebrity, unfortunately.

She had started off being a household name and **then** had tried to communicate her art: that's how the public understood it. In fact, it hadn't been like that at all. She had started off as an artist.

Music wasn't something she had happened on after she met Lennon. She was playing piano and studying composition when she was five.

By the time she went to New York's Sarah Lawrence School she was interested in composing music that challenged; she was looking for complexity. And so she wrote songs with complex chords that would be difficult for people to sing.

With the "Fly" album she was trying to expand certain possibilities of form. With this one she was hoping to communicate with people who would understand her lyrics, mainly.

"Musically, I felt like I had 2,000 miles of emotion and I was a long distance runner. I just went through that distance. To cover it I went the most functional route, just running."

She had got to the point where she needed to communicate to people who would understand her. With a song like "What A Bastard", which on one level deals with the situation

of a woman whose man has walked out on her, she was conscious of trying to get across to housewives.

I wondered if, by becoming more accessible, she felt she had compromised any of those original concepts and values.

She laughed and said it was very symbolic, it was a double album. If it had been a single it would have been a more commercial proposition because with a double sales were right away cut in half.

But she wrote enough for a triple album, which she'd decided against, so she had compromised in a way.

"I'm not worried about being more communicative in the conventional sense. I think it's a good sign because I can see myself as being sort of a snob in a way."

She meant intellectually, and I asked her if there was ever any conflict between her and John over their respective backgrounds—hers Harvard and artistically and intellectually elitist, his essentially that of a pop musician. Friends, for instance.

Not really, she replied. John had begun in art school, so he had that background, and he was already sophisticated enough to understand that side of life.

And her friends were certainly interested in talking to John, not just because he was John Lennon, but because of shared interests and subjects, like extra sensory perception, say.

"From my point of view I was just getting sick and tired of the pseudo intellectual, elitist atmosphere of the circle I was in, in London. I was thinking, 'am I gonna end up as the Queen Mother of the avant garde world, always meeting these snobs talking about elitist kicks?' and I was starting to feel frightened.

"When I started to make the 'Bottoms' film I became very known in England in a strange sort of way—like to taxi drivers, that sort of thing—and my elite friends were so very upset about that. They were saying, 'well, she copped out, she went commercial or something'.

"They thought it was a very vulgar move to make.

"I said, it's great to communicate your art with the working class, what is this? But all the same they stopped inviting me to their tea party; just sort of inverted snobbery.

"Around this time I met John. The first song we recorded on this album was 'Song for John' and it was a song I made actually before I met him. I was hoping to find somebody who'd fly with me, or whatever, and I made a demo record.

"In those days Island Records was interested in letting me do whatever I wanted to do, which is sort of avant garde music. I was thinking maybe it's a good idea to include one or two straight songs on it and I made this demo.

"It's the first demo of mine that John listened to when he visited me, and that's why, for sentimental reasons, I called it 'Song For John' later. It's the same tune, same lyrics."

Long before she met Lennon, therefore, she had acquired the knack of needling people, of forcing them, however unconsciously, to take sides.

It still goes on much the same as ever, of course. She says that the sensitive people who wish them nice things are too shy to come forward, so the ones they're always facing, the ones that say things like "you Jap bastard", come across better, if that's the word.

Against all this flak, she said, one could react in two ways. One was to be extremely callous about everything, forget the muckstirrer and escape from the world.

The other was to become someone like Pat Nixon, and hide behind a smile: those people who are so afraid they don't speak a word, or if they do, make sure it doesn't mean anything. I didn't think the Lennons fitted either of these categories.

Speaking of Pat Nixon, I asked her what woman she identified with, if at all. Well, she replied, John had been saying they were Scott and Zelda, and she had come to the point before the album where she was thinking, yes, I am Zelda, because if I don't make this record I'm going to go insane.

"As an artist, if you have 20 ideas in your mind and for many reasons you feel you shouldn't make it, then you go crazy".

But the Fitzgeralds were victims, weren't they?

" Yes, we have that side, we have that side. In a way we were going to be that and we overcame it. Now it's the past".

So what women, I repeated, did she identify with?

" Joan of Arc, maybe", and she gave a small laugh.

But she was another victim.

"I know, but is there any woman who isn't? I can't identify with past female figures, because they're mostly victims, and I really think I belong to the next generation."

So did she see herself spearheading a whole feminist revolution?

"I think that crusading stuff the militant feminists are doing is a bit skin deep in a way. I do understand their point but I was trying to bring out the side that was deeper than that.

"You can't say, 'let's dispense with all men and shove them into a slave house or whatever'. Then the problem isn't over.

"With lesbianism and whatever, all women are tempted to avoid a meeting with men at this point because we've been suffering so much, so it's easy to say, 'well, men are all pigs, let's just get on, without them'. I think it's like an escape."

Even with two women, I said, one of them would assume a male role.

"That's a possibility, too, oh yes, and many women are getting into that trap. I know lesbians who say, look at those tits, they're just too good for pigs', so they're commenting on sisters like they were pigs themselves."

But when she talked of moving society in a more feminine direction, what did she mean by "more feminine?"

Most artists, she explained, were already very feminine. With the conventional idea of masculinity/femininity, masculinity was supposed to be the symbol of power and competition.

And women weren't competitive?

"Well, we're masculists, most of us. In other words, the only reason we get accepted in this society at all is to use the same game that men use, to get there and be approved by the male society.

"I mean, men say, if you want to be equal you gotta go to war, but not really, because if we bring out the feminine side of society nobody wants war." India, I retorted, had a woman as prime minister, and her female population was nothing if not subjugated.

"The reason is they have a masculist female as a prime minister. Because it's a masculine society, most women who make it are not any kinder to women at all, they're just like other men.

"It's amazingly similar to black society. The blacks who've made it in white society have sold their souls to the point of being white, actually. They look black, but they're white inside.

"That's why society is so perverted. They plant in you the idea that unless you're aggressive you're gonna die or fail, and everyone is so insecure they're always trying to exert power . . ."

At this point I leaned across and lit her cigarette. I asked if my action offended her.

"No, no", she replied airily, "I light men's cigarettes too. I think it's just being friendly."

But in New York, I continued, where homosexuality of both kinds was very overt, women seemed to be emasculating many heterosexual men.

Ah, she said, but the statistics showed that men were getting more impotent, anyway—caused by severe, neurotic competition, she supposed, between themselves. The more impotent they became the more they had to compensate by seeking political power; it was a vicious circle.

She stopped. She didn't want to pursue the conversation along the line of politics. The immigration problem, she murmured. We talked about New York.

They liked living there, she said, because compared to other cities it was pretty liberal, not just for women but for mixed, racial marriages, like theirs. England was basically a WASP society. Only when you went to a restaurant did you see foreigners—and they were the cooks and waiters.

I asked her if she and John were happy people. Not necessarily, she replied, but she said it lightly.

"Sometimes we're very happy, sometimes we're not. We're human. There was a negative situation at one time, like Scott and Zelda, but we overcame that because we were a bit more aware, thank God.

"Maybe I'm stronger than Zelda and John is a bit more aware than Scott, or because we live in a more aware age.

"Being two artists living together, we're doing pretty well considering."

She smiled. It was a nice smile. It had an air of optimism.

Rock and Roll Women

Bette Midler

by Roy Hollingworth

My passion for Bette Midler began quite a while ago.

It began, I remember on a clammy New York evening. A sweaty audience in the open-air Woolman Rink, Central Park, fidgeted, swigging Coke and Shaeffer beer. Then SHE appeared, all breasts and lips and movement. High on a stage, hands on hips that bumped like nobody had ever bumped before. Eyes began to goggle.

She sang feminine songs, and fetching songs, and although the sound-system was frayed and a mite tattered . . . she was just a woman, and as the legend now reads . . . divine.

So it seemed a bit strange, in the back of a cold London cab, inching its way forward to the Churchill Hotel. It seemed strange because since I'd last seen her . . . she had become a "star". No longer the prize possession of naughty New York City—God bless that wicked place.

I'd put a suit on, and resorted to Marlboro ciggies again. Suits and Marlboro's were a New York habit.

Somehow I wanted it to be New York. For some reason Bette didn't figure being here.

"Room 623, and ask for Miss Russo, and don't bring a photographer"—so spake Warner Bros. Oh, oh, the whole star bit.

Immediate flashes went through my brain: Bette lounging like a silken snake across a 10ft long settee, covered in scents and furry things, smoking St. Moritz with the help of a long, black cigarette holder. The flashes continued as the elevator silently rose past the fourth floor.

Should I have brought flowers? Would I have to sit on the floor? Album reviews, and previous interviews ran through my mind. This whole *"divine Miss M."* thing. Room 623, I knocked once.

Dear Annie Ivil of Warner Bros opened the door, and I was ushered in. A large suite to be sure—but certainly not gross. Without making it look obvious my eyes searched the room for *her.*

She wasn't there. There were only three people in the room, and she wasn't there. Possibly munching caviar on the toilet I thought. Maybe she's sleeping, and "vants to be left alone."

And then the shock. "This is Bette," said Annie, introducing me to the figure on the settee. Jeez, I thought it was a bloke. "Oh, hi there, pleased to meet you," I fumbled for words. Was this a joke?

It was a large nose, and a heavily and lumpily scupltured Jewish face that met with my gaze. It was her.

She ripped a smallish scarf off her head, to display a headful of steel curlers. Her sweater was baggy, but glancing for a second time, I knew something was moving inside there. She wore jeans, and well, that was it.

"Oh, I'm so dry," she said. I couldn't think of an answer to that one. I didn't really know what she meant. She walked over to the fridge, and produced a bottle of Perrier water, poured a whole big glass, and chugged it down.

She fell on to the settee again, and smiled.

I was given a bottle of beer—but I felt stifled. Well, ask her what her measurements are. How would that one go? I thought.

She was doing something with her nails—looking at them I think. She'd turn round and smile, but looked dull, and ugly in her curlers.

"What are your measurements"— it slipped out like a belch after a gassy meal. I didn't know I'd done it

until I'd done it—if you see what I mean.

Silence.

Annie Ivil, who was flitting about the room stopped—looked at me, and looked at Bette . . . Who looked at Annie, and then looked at me.

Like magic her whole appearance changed. The face, which, as I said before, looked ugly, suddenly, remodelled itself. Muscles began to work; her eyes opened wide, and her lips spread, and she crossed her legs, and lounged back, hands behind her head.

"What . . . my boy? *What?*"

"Uhmmm, your measurements. What are your measurements?"

"I'm embarrassed," said Annie Ivil. "I'm not going to look."

Bette was curling, and snaking into another pose. Now **she** was not embarrassed. **I** was, she knew that.

"I'm 40 . . . (long pause) . . . 22 . . . (longer pause) . . . 36."

She didn't say anything else, but preened herself like a peacock, as much as to say. "Howz that boysie, yer satisfied?"

I was.

"But I'm only 2ft 5in. high," she continued, and burst into laughter.

Atmosphere broken.

She'd been to see George Melly the night before, somewhere in the Surrey country. She'd ended up on stage with him. "He was just lovely. I'd like to see him wear earrings. Oh he's *so* bizarre."

And what are you, Bette?

"Well . . . (long pause, she mimes a schoolgirl modest look of shyness and embarrassment) . . . Well, I just sings my brains out and shake my tits."

I know.

"You've seen me."

Yes, New York.

"O thank God somebody over here has seen me. You know everyone who's come to interview me has expected to see this *divine* woman of *intense* beauty. And here I am baby, sat in my curlers and jeans, and *this* is *me* baby."

When she said the word *me,* she thrust her breasts forward, and even the baggy sweater gave way to that pair of loaded 40s.

I remained unmoved (liar) . . . calm (liar) . . . and coolly reached for a cigarette (liar). I fumbled for the pack, she knew I was fumbling—she reached them first, and offered me them.

"As I said," she said. "This is me, and that divine lady up on stage is me too baby."

Which one is the *real* you? (I slipped into the New York habit of emphasising certain words).

"I like them both a whole lot, and I miss each of them when I'm without the other."

We talked about the New York concert. A lot had happened since then.

"It's all very strange," she said, guzzling more Perrier water, and curling into a pose, this time messy. "There are so many options now. So many things being offered to me. So much happening to me. But I still remain the same old Bette. I just want to be me. I don't want to fall into that old showbiz trap of believing my critics. How could I, my dear—just look at me.

"I have to be realistic when it comes down to fame. I have to look beyond that. I have to look to what's really important, and that's just getting up on stage, and singing my damned head off, and shaking these damned things." She shook *them* just a little—they took a while to shiver to a halt.

"I just want to sing to people. I don't want any crap surrounding that simple fact.

"I regard every gig as a party— and I'm the hostess. I have to keep people happy, keep them moving, keep them entertained."

But a lot of people say that they'll never be taken in by fame. And yet . . . most of them fall to the wicked disease it throws up—I aimed that one at her.

"Look, if the crap started growing around me. If it all became too big, then I would just go back to my little circle of clubs and friends, and be very happy to go back. I have a lot of friends. And I love them."

Bette has been singing for about four years now, and has meddled with theatre since she was 15. She was brought up on what she calls "The Great Women"—Sarah Bernhardt, Lorette Taylor.

"Now they were just fabulous. Then they were women. I wanted to grow, and live in their lives, and I wanted to live a life like they did. But I was forced out of that dream, and into another—i.e. what's happening to me now."

Do you feel anybody lives like The Great Women did. I mean, could they happen now?

"I don't know. Maybe, but not in the real way" . . . she stopped talking, and made for a chair in the centre of the room. For a while she sat quite normally, and then started posing, one hand on hip—the other behind her head. Her chin up, a proud look upon her now delicious looking face. "And then . . . . . there was Greta Garbo. Oh Greta Garbo."

Who did she like in the contemporary field? Did she like Ray Davies, did she like Legs Larry Smith?

"Legs Larry, Oh, Legs Larry, Oh I love him. I'd love to do something with him. I saw him at a party in New York, I saw him, and just wanted to go up to him, and be near him. And Ray Davies, I love him, too.

"I love 'Lola,' and 'All Day And All Of The Night' I really want to sing those songs."

She started singing "Lola," slowly, emphasising each word, pushing her hair up from behind (the curlers had now gone, and this bouncing red-head had come into life).

She went to the toilet, and when she returned the questions didn't flow quite so easily.

Um, what do you do in your spare time?

"I get high, and listen to music."

The talk drifted towards New York. "I arrived seven years ago—that was just when Mayor Lindsay took office. I've watched the police force out of control. I've watched the police force and fire brigade, and everything fall out of Lindsay's control. I've watched it become a mind-bending place — but would never desert it.

"I look upon New York as my mission in life. To leave that City would be abandoning my mission. I'd resent myself if I walked out on the place.

"I pick up rubbish in the Park, I don't drop crap on the sidewalks. I tell people to try and stop it all falling to pieces. That's what I do. That's my mission.

"There's music happening there—New York music—and I regard myself as being part of that. There's always hope. I believe there will be a cultural revival in New York. I have to be optimistic—we all do.

"I'm not going to sell my apartment there. Where did you live in New York?"

Um, Sutton Place (a flash area).

"Oh, you . . . Oh! Hey, they didn't tell me you were the *big* paper. Oh my gosh. Oh, now what can I say!"

She began to fuss, and in a beautifully funny way.

As you like Davies, Legs Larry, and Melly, can you see a revival of a more music-hall/Hollywood/show-bizzy style to contemporary enter-tainment?

"Oh yes, but I don't know if I'm really in the same field as those people."

I feel you are. You don't do concerts—you do shows.

"Is there a difference?" she asked.

Yes. A show is . . . er . . . a show. A concert is just walking on stage, and well, taking it from there.

"Oh, I see what you mean. Yes, I do shows. I mean that's me. Sure I'm into *theatre* my dear. Theatre is so *fabulous*. I believe people love it."

Her fascination for Legs Larry continued. "I want to see him, oh I want to see him."

An hour had passed, and now she was Bette Midler. She was posing, and pouting, and having a load of fun with herself. Now she was in a constant movie scene. Each word she uttered was accompanied by a flutter of the eyelids, a wave of the hand, a quick shudder of her breasts, a tossing of the head.

"So, sure we're aiming back into showbiz with rock. But let's always remember something important—your music has gotta be as good as that show.

"Sure I know just everybody is dressing up on stage now. But you've got to do it *right* darling.

"I you're gonna put fabulous clothes on darling then you've gotta do something fabulous inside those clothes. Dig?

"Tina Turner does it. She does *everything*. When I saw her, I got up, and said 'dear, look what that woman is doing. She's doing *everything*.' I came out of her concert feeling wasted. Now that's how you should leave a concert. You should limp out and feel wasted."

The Stones?

We talked of the incredible Madison Square Garden concert of last year. She'd been there.

"I got outa my seat, and I stood in the aisle, and I saw just what that Mick Jagger was doing. I saw just what he was doing. You know what I mean—he was doing '*it*'—right there on stage."

Doing what?

"It my darling. Oh the nerve. I stood there and I shouted '*please* . . . *Oh please*.'

"Oh how I wanted *him*."

More Perrier water flowed. She opened the fridge for another bottle. The fridge was stacked high with Perrier water. She shimmied back to her seat, tossed her hair back.

"I'm a very opinionated young lady. I have my opinions about things. And mine are the only correct ones. Dig?"

She walked into the bathroom.

"Gonna get this little lady fixed up for tonight. Gonna make me divine."

She began to laugh.

"How could I ever change. I'm me. As I said before—as soon as I see me being changed, then I'm going away from it all. All I want is people."

Hype? You must be damned well joking. Bette Midler is Bette Midler. *A star, my darlings.*

Carly Simon keeps a sun-kissed apartment in Manhattan, but her heart lies in Martha's Vineyard, the resort island off Cape Cod, Massachusetts.

She and her husband, James Taylor, are looking forward to the completion of their house up there by the end of the year.

"The best place of the house", says Carly Simon with a smile as pleased and bright as on the back of her album "No Secrets", "is we have a 45 foot tower with four storeys and just a circular stairway going up to the top. On the top you're so close to the stars".

Carly's apartment is that rare kind where there are plenty of soft couches to flop down on.

The only touch of disorder is her opened suitcase on the living room floor next to a high, intricately constructed, but still unfinished table that James built the previous evening.

She hates to unpack and might as well not bother because she's taking off with James for his Japanese tour and one Hawaiian concert in a few days. She herself has no plans to

perform except for a TV special to be taped in the spring.

"I do want to do some things with James", she says.

"I'll probably work myself into his show in Japan in devious little ways. I don't know how but I mean he invited me to. It's not that I'm usurping his time. In a way I'd prefer not to perform. I like to avoid feeling uncomfortable.

"When I perform I feel that much more uncomfortable than normally but I probably will work into his show a little bit. When we come back from Japan he'll probably be doing a week's worth of concerts all around the United States and then that will be it for performing for him for a while.

"I have trouble at performing now because the album is very produced and I would feel naked without everybody who played on it being there. It's a very full sound and I'd like to duplicate it".

To anyone who's seen Carly work, it must seem incredible that she doesn't like to perform. She comes across as one of the most

natural, most loving and most relaxed performers I've ever seen. A woman who enjoys herself and wants the audience to do the same.

Still, she says: "I don't know a performer, with the exception of maybe John McLaughlin, who's not terrified to go onstage, but everybody deals with it in a different way.

"There are some people who deal with their fear by almost turning their back on the audience—not literally, but who need to have that much distance between themselves and the audience so they don't really communicate in trying to convince themselves there's no audience there.

"My way of dealing with it is to include the audience in whatever is going on. The only way that I can overcome my sense of fear is to have us all be one, is to almost have a feeling that they're up onstage with me. They're part of my act. But, it's out of fear. I wish it wasn't.

"When I made my first album I wasn't going to perform at all. I was just going to make an album. I didn't even have a manager.

"My first single which was 'That's

Rock and Roll Women

Carly Simon

by Loraine Alterman

The Way I've Always Heard It To Be' got on the charts and Elektra was quite right in wanting me to go out and promote it.

"So I got the opportunity to play the Troubadour with Cat Stevens and it was an offer I couldn't refuse".

Ask Carly if she's begun working on her next album yet and she answers with a smile in a Maria Ouspenskaya Transylvanian gypsy accent: "My dear, I just completed this vun".

Then she gets serious and explains: "I refuse to be propelled in the typical way that singers are in this business, like if you've got a hit you've got to follow it up quick with a follow-up single.

"Of course, its the way it goes. Just grind them out. I can't do it. I just know I can't.

"Perhaps this is my peak and from now on it will be downhill, but if that's the way it's got to be—I've got to keep my health and my mental health and my homelife and the things that are more important to me than having hit records".

But when she does her next album, she hopes it will once more be done in her favourite place to live—England.

"Being away from New York is very important for me when I'm making a record or doing any work because I can concentrate", she says.

"Being in New York means answering the telephone all the time, means paying homage to all of my friends and family that I've known for years. Lots of social obligations. I can hardly even write in New York. This is just a place to stop over and send my clothes to the cleaners.

"England is great because I don't know that many people over there and when I'm going over there, I'm going there just to work and any non-working activities that come along are mere surprises".

Despite the social pulls of New York, Carly did manage to write most of the songs on her last album here, but says:

"I'm very good on moving vehicles which are a good place for me to write. I wrote 'Loving You's The Right Thing To Do' coming down on the plane from Martha's Vine-

yard. I wrote 'We Have No Secrets' and the line 'clouds in my coffee' from 'You're So Vain' on a plane. I wrote several songs on my first album on trains—that was when I wouldn't fly.

"Moving vehicles are all very good for lyrical inspirations. I've never written any melodies other than at home because I've had to have a piano or guitar."

More and more Carly's been writing on the piano. An upright with the insides exposed sits against her living room wall.

She explains: "I'm more inspired by the piano because I'm really not a very good guitarist. I'm not really a very good pianist either.

"I don't mean to put myself down but I get thwarted by my own inability to do more on a guitar. On the piano I need less dexterity so you can just kind of sit down and almost go like that".

She arranges both hands in imaginary chords and clunks them down in the air, and then continues: "Even if it's a mistake, it might come out nicely. I didn't start playing the piano until two years ago and now I'm just playing all the time.

"I love the piano. I can tell that that's going to be my major instrument although James and I just bought some little recorders and we've been learning how to play them. We've been playing duets".

So far the two of them have not collaborated on any songs and Carly says: "I think we're capable of doing all kinds of things together and it will probably take a while because we're so newly in love that it's very hard to do anything except for just being in love.

"I mean that takes up a great deal of our time, just that state of being, which is so beautiful now. It's really great. Whereas we do play music together and sing together, it's not in a really professional capacity. We don't have a show to plan together or anything like that".

Several songs on each of Carly's album have been written with Jacob Brackman whom Carly met in 1967. She calls him the turning point in her professional life because he encouraged her to write and sing more.

They've written together since 1970, but at the moment Brackman has disappeared in Jamaica where he's immersed in a Sufi training programme and solitude. Carly hopes he'll turn up again to write with her even though they don't do that much work together.

"I've never spent an evening with Jake just writing", she says.

"The way we do it is I give him a melody on tape and he sets lyrics to it. For the first time on this last album we reversed that and he gave me a set of lyrics for 'The Carter Family'. Other than that it's always been that I give him the melody.

"He's just amazing. He's really uncanny the way he comes up with lyrics that fit the melody so well. I've never known another lyricist that can do that so well. And such intricate words.

"Jake is not one to write anything clicheish, anything even remotely obvious. Jake is really an interesting writer and the lyrics that he comes up with are very special".

As a lyricist herself, Carly's songs very often seem very revealing about her own life and so she's really opening up her innermost feelings to strangers.

"Just as when you're reading a novel, you don't know if it's autobiographical or if the person just has a very lively imagination. I think anything that comes from your imagination is as personal as anything that comes from your real life.

"So that no matter if you're writing from your imagination or from fact, it's still extremely personal. It's still opening yourself up.

"I think there are probably lots of people who would try very hard to get away from anything that directly concerned them, but I don't feel the need to do that at all. I mean, so what!

"Of course, anything that I write is terribly, terribly personal, even if it's like 'Embrace Me You Child'. It was originally called 'Night Time Songs'. That's a song that I consider that I was the go-between the power that inspired it and what finally came out.

"It's the only song that I've ever written that I've seemed to have no control over, that my hand almost led, that I didn't think it out, I didn't have any idea for that song.

"I'd been talking with my friend and lead guitarist Jimmy Ryan and I said, 'Jimmy, I just can't seem to write anything. I'm all dried up'. Every writer feels that from time to time.

"He said, 'I won't hear that from you. You've got to sit down and write no matter how painful or how little time you have. You can do it'.

"So that evening Jimmy left and he put up a little sign that he made me sign on my bulletin board saying 'I will write whether or not it's inconvenient, time consuming, etc., etc.'

"That evening", she continues, I just kind of sat down without any ideas for a song and that song just kind of came out of me.

"I mean usually I have a couple of ideas in planning, an idea germinating, building up and all, a little line here and a little line there. I'll say, 'Oh gee, that line would go nicely in there'. But this song just really kind of flowed right from me. But that's no more personal than a song that I've been perfunctory about".

Fat Fred and Patsy

by Roy Hollingworth

At 164 North Gower Street, London, lives a company by the name of Artists' Services.

The legend, "The Complete Service", runs across the company's card. Twelve years ago they were just a smallish company that supplied limousines and drivers for "artistes" of any calibre.

Now they supply something else. They are The Protectors. They supply "protection" for artists. They "look after" some of the biggest acts in the business, and "look after" those who would like to invade the privacy, or safety of the afore-mentioned artistes.

At the Bowie concert at Earls Court, for instance, Artists' Services had 100 men there to make sure that Mr. Bowie was not "done over"; to make sure the stage was not invaded; to make sure the kids didn't stampede themselves to death.

One hundred men—most of them just hired for the night. They were all big men. You have to be big.

I'd like to tell you about two of those men—Fat Fred and Patsy.

Unlike the bulk of those there at Bowie's Earls Court do, Fat Fred and Patsy had the "big jobs". You see, they're pro-men. They're employed full-time by the company. They're a team. They're always together. And after more than a decade together, they have a tale to tell.

I first met up with "the lads" in the glamorous surroundings of the drinking lounge of London's Heathrow Airport. They were being flown out to re-join Led Zeppelin. Destination: George V Hotel, Paris. Not a bad step-up for these lads who were brought up in the sour streets of East London. They quaffed light and bitters.

They were doing pretty much the same recently when I caught up with them in their more "at home" surroundings—a London pub.

Fat Fred—age 27, weight 20 stones, 5ft 9in, married. He has a face of rich fatness and humour, and kindness. He's all rosied up, and sweating a bit. You might say he had a baby face actually. Despite his extra tonnage, he looks as healthy as a freshly picked plum.

Patsy: age 28, weight 15 stones, height 5ft 9in. Real name is actually Patsy Collins. A hard face that's seen a lot, and felt a bit too. A few scars litter his forehead. A really thick East End accent. Fat Fred is open with his humour—Patsy is dry, incredibly funny, and married with a kid, and another on the way.

Like Fred, he looks very "healthy".

They were just sinking a few lunchtime gallons. They'd got "a job on" that night—Pink Floyd at Earls Court. "Shouldn't be much trouble", says Fred. "No, you're right", adds Patsy, "I 'ear the Floyd lot just sits and listens to the music". He rolls a cigarette, and tugs at his bitter. "But we'll be there . . . just to keep an eye on 'em".

'Em?

"Well", says Fred, "'em is the stage, those on it, and those watchin' it".

And how long have they been watching 'em?

"Well", says Patsy, "it started when The Monkees come over. The company then was just sort of car hire, but The Monkees wanted a bit of security like. So we had 12 on the job didn't we Fred?"

Fred: "Yeh".

"And, 'er we was wiv the boys 24 hours a day. You know we slept in the same hotels, and got really close to them", continued Patsy. "And they liked this kind of security. You know, it was different. We weren't plodderin' old boys in blue uniforms. They could do anythin' they liked in front of us. It was as though we was one of them".

Before joining Artists' Services Patsy spent most of his time "totting". He had a van, and picked up scrap and the like.

"Did a bit of decorating too", he added. "Well, I'd sort of do anyfin for a bit of money". Fred was in pretty much the same way. They weren't even into music—not until they did the Monkees "job".

What sort of things happened with The Monkees?

Fred: "Well, it was a very good first lesson".

Patsy: "Yeh, it really was. I mean let's take one night. There was about 5,000 kids outside the hotel, and they were tryin' every possible way to get in. Jesus, they were a fearless bunch. We had to be around every minute. It's exactly the same as it is now with Cassidy and the Osmonds".

You worked with the Osmonds didn't you?

"Yeh", they both breathed, and shook their heads.

"Those fans of theirs", said Patsy, "they was so bleedin' wise. They knew every move the band was makin'. I mean our prime concern always is to look after the artists, but with the Osmonds our main time was cut out lookin' after the bleedin' kids.

"Take when they was tryin' to leave the hotel. We make sure the lads get into the car okay, and then, Jesus, we have to pull girls back who are about to throw themselves under the bleedin' car. They were trying to jump on it while it was movin' and we were savin' their bleedin' little lives".

"And they didn't like that one little bit", added Fred. "They were tearin' at us, and going bloody crazy, and we're tryin' to protect them from getting a two ton limo runnin' over their 'eads.

"Jesus", continues Fred, "I'd rather face fellas than face those Osmonds fans!"

"Yeh", agrees Patsy.

"I mean Patsy, wiv a fella you can just go up to 'im and say 'stop', with a bit of aggression like. And if he don't stop, you can say 'stop' again, and make your presence felt a bit. But wiv those kids. You say 'now look 'ere youngster', and before you know it, she's run between yer legs. There's no way of controllin' 'em".

What methods do you use to "control" a crowd?

Patsy: "Well, we have a sort of code. You know, if you ask somebody to stop, and they don't, then you tell 'em to stop. And then if they still don't stop . . . er . . . you do somethin' about it. We always make a point of arskin' first though, then tellin'. It's not all brawn you know, you got to use yer loaf. No, we always arsk 'em first".

What was the next "big job" after The Monkees?

Fred: "Er, it was the Blind Faith do in Hyde Park. Yeh, that was a big one—about half a million bleedin' people there".

Patsy: "Yeh, we worked alongside The Hell's Angels. You know, we gev 'em a bit of a talkin' to, and they decided to work with us—and not against us. I saw there was a load of 'em standin' around the front of the stage complainin'. I asks them what's the matter, they says they can't see. So I says, well there's a lot of others can't see neither, so are you going to help us get everyone sat down?

"And the Angels say 'right', and we did it.

"Yeh, after the show", continued Patsy, "the Angels had bin so good that we had a drink wiv 'em.

"It's a case of talkin' to people, not hittin' 'em—talkin' to them".

You don't see yourselves as just being bouncers then?

"No, oh no", they both replied.

"I mean look. We've been to concerts, and we've seen the old style bouncer in action. You know, we've seen kids leapin' on the stage, and we've seen the old boys just kick them off—and really kick them. They don't care about the kids, they've got their money for the night, and that's all they care about.

"Our way of thinkin' is that we protect everybody. Christ we don't want to see people get . . . er . . . kicked".

My mind flashes back to the Zeppelin gig in Paris. For some foolish reason, I'd left the back stage area, and had a wander around the massive stadium. I then tried to get backstage again.

After leaping over the barriers—somewhat idiotically — I was "roughed up" a bit by two French bouncers. They were just about to really cobble me, when Fred appeared. In strong English he politely told the French to put me down. They took one look at Fred . . . and put me down.

"I mean look", says Fred, "we did the Fats Domino job the other week, and you know who's there causin' the trouble? Only the bleedin' police. They was manhandlin' these old rockers, and hittin' 'em, and pushin' them down. We told the police they were wrong, and that we were the security, and we could look after things. I mean nobody gets past us. They don't. And it's very rarely that anyone has to get hit".

Patsy: "I mean we saw that they was rockers at this gig, and we knew there was no way they were goin' to just sit in their seats to see Fats. Man, they wanted to dance. And our way of thinkin' is 'let 'em', I mean, why shouldn't they?

"There's no way you're gonna say to 'em, er 'sit down the Queen will be on in a minute'. They're rockers, and they want to rock. So you just tell 'em to have a good time, but keep it cool, and don't get on the stage. And they understand you know.

"They were good as gold, dancing away, and then the police arrive, and before you know it, there's a load of scuffles goin' on . . . and its all a mess."

Who else have you worked with?

Fred (sweating away): "Well, we've been working pretty steadily with Zeppelin for the past four years. Then there's bin Andy Williams, Johnny Cash, the Osmonds . . . And, er, the Russians".

The Russians?

"Yeh", says Fred with pride.

"The Russian gymnast team that came over. I was lookin' after that little piece Olga, and Patsy had some world champion. I had to take Olga shoppin' and the like. She fell for me I think".

"Right", laughs Patsy, "she really did. She thought Fred was lovely. Well, the whole team thought we was both okay. They gev us medals and things when they left, and had us pose with them on most of the photos".

What's the most frightening thing that's ever happened to you both?

"When I got stabbed, really stabbed", said Fred.

Where was that?

"That was on the continent with Zeppelin last month.

"Yeh, it's a different story with Zep. I mean, when we're with Zep we're REALLY security men. We have to be. With the Osmonds we're more sort of 'public relations men'."

"But you get on the Continent with Zep, and it's somethin' else", said Patsy.

What do you mean?

"Well, there's just no way with the kids over there. I mean they have these militant movements who seem to just want to go along, and fight. Now we're in this business to look after people, and to be able to do that we've got to be able to look after ourselves. So if they pick a fight with us, then they've picked the wrong bleedin' people. Right Fred?"

"Right".

"Take one episode with Zep", says Patsy. "There was this geezer up on the lights. You know he's climbed the lighting tower. So I asks him to come down. He does. Then I sees him up there again. So I asks him to come down. Then he's up there again. So I calls him down, and I puts on a stern face like, and I say 'for f . . . sake don't climb up there agen'. Then his mates come back wiv him, and they're like showing their fists. I mean there was no way out then. If I turns me back they'd be on me. So I . . . er . . . wallop one. And . . . er . . . when they've seen yer wallop one, they . . . er . . . stop. 'Cause when it comes to the crunch you've got to make one blow really count. You've got to make it final".

And now, my friends, the Copenhagen story.

It was here that Fred and Patsy had their most awful night. Even before Zeppelin got on stage, a load of youths were on too. Fred and bold Patsy managed to talk the situation into some sort of control. "We were tellin' 'em to get off, and they was comin' back wiv this funny language, we get an interpreter, and well, they get off".

So all was fine, and Zep played the show, and there was no trouble. Fred and Patsy see the band into their cars, and they're left alone in the car park. On turning round to get their car they see a half-moon of guys waiting for them.

"Yeh, they stood there—about five or six of 'em, and they were sayin' they was goin' to do us. Well, we done four of them, and then a load more appears, and like we stunned 'em agen".

"Yeh, stunned 'em", says Fred.

"And yeh another six stunned, and there's a load more appears . . ."

You'd already stunned quite a few hadn't you?

"Well, they're all lip over there . . . It's pretty easy".

Back to the story.

In fact another 20 youths appeared, and even fighting like fury Fred and Patsy were over-run. Fred was stabbed in the back, and Patsy met with a chunk of iron on the front of his head, and back.

"We lay there for a bit, and then got up, and they'd gone.

"I mean, we *got up*, and went back to the hotel. I mean, if say four of us got on to two of them, *they wouldn't get up*. Know what I mean?"

Fred didn't actually know he'd been stabbed until somebody pointed it out to him back at the hotel. Zeppelin were a bit panicky about what had happened, and flew out of Copenhagen a day early.

"I think they did that because of us. But we was okay the next morning, all stitched up and ready for the next job. We were back humpin' a few suitcases.

"In fact", added Patsy, "we look back on that little episode as a joke . . . y'know, it 'ad us in stitches!"

There was this time at a New York concert when a security man dealt me one blow and I fell 12 foot off a stage, and into New Jersey City Hospital with concussion. "Now that's bad", says Fred, looking at me. "He should have arsked yer first. Know what I mean. Some people just don't have any brain . . . and we do".

Do you feel a rock band could exist these days without your sort of protection? Could Zeppelin play Paris without somebody like you about?

"No, oh no", says Patsy.

"We're a vital part of the show now", adds Fred. "I mean there are too many extremists about now for a rock band to be able to play without special security.

"Let's put it this way. There was this time in Paris when a roadie threw a chick right off stage—that's ten feet high, and a hard floor. Bonzo (Bonham) was furious—the roadie was sacked on the spot. We found the chick, and apart from a bit of a bloodied nose she was okay—miraculously. Robert Plant stopped the show, and brought the girl on stage to show everyone she was okay. We'd missed the incident by a few seconds. Now you don't throw people off stages like that. You take them off, as we would have done".

A lot of things went wrong at the Bowie thing at Earls Court. Why couldn't people see? Why was there that whole rushing scene at the front?

"Well, they're teething troubles. I mean it's the first time they've put rock on there. There had to be teething troubles. I mean there was 100 of us, and 18,000 of them".

That's only 1,800 each lads.

"Er, that's just overdoin' it a little bit", says Fred.

"All it wanted was barriers across the aisles. God knows why they didn't think of doing that. God knows. You see once those kids had rushed, there was no way of stoppin' them. But it won't happen again.

"I mean I never even saw Bowie", says Fred. "I was lookin' after the backstage, and every bloody second there was somebody running through".

"You see the thing about this business", says Patsy, "is that if nothing happens at a concert, you won't hear a thing about it in the papers. And that means you've had good security. If somethin' does happen, there's all sorts of people blamed, but they can't see that they've had incredible security, and without it, there would have been a total riot. If we do our job properly, and there's enough of us there you'll never notice us".

They lead a strange life. They have to blend into every band they work with. Now the Osmonds don't drink or smoke. So Fred and Patsy had to drop the drink and smokes.

"Got on very well with the lads—but a bit thirsty at times".

It's okay in Britain say the lads. But the Continent?

"There's little hope that it'll get any better. We had a guy come back the other day. He said the whole audience had demanded to get into this gig for nothing. This winds up with the whole security force being cut up and everythin'. I mean when we was with Zep, you see kids who've paid £3 to get in, spitting at Zep's car, and kickin' it. Jesus, they're crazy.

"There's a gang over in Germany —a load of gangsters who just go to every gig, and smash up everythin'. Well, we'd heard about them, and before this gig we goes and finds them, and 'as a little talk to them, and hires them. They were well pleased to be hired. And they were good as gold".

"We seem to have a magic touch", says Fred.

"You see when you go to any place, and when you see the local troublemakers there, the only way to stop them makin' trouble is to employ 'em. Soon shuts 'em up", says Patsy.

They're the ace boys with the firm then?

"Well, there's others in this company who are bigger than us, but when a rough job comes up—it's US in charge. I mean, we were both brought up in the streets, and we were built for it. Dig?

"We're different from the old style boy who just wanted £10 for a night, and a good fight. We don't. We get the idiots who come up and say 'come on', and they want a fight. And we say 'no'. And they really want one, but then they takes a look at us, and suddenly they think they'd be better off without a fight. See what I mean?

"We're a bit cunnin'. I mean we have to change, and adapt so much. I mean Cassidy one week, Osmonds the next, then Robert Plant, then Johnny Cash, and then the bleedin' Russians".

You're born actors, I add.
"Yeh, right".

Now look, you were brought up in the streets. Now you get the star treatment at star hotels. I mean, stayin' at the George V, Paris, is a bit different from The Bull, Hackney. Has this business altered that East End earthiness?

"We couldn't have starry eyes for too long, we knew that", says Fred. "But we had them for a while. I mean, meetin' the stars and stayin' at the George The Sank, and the 'Ilton Amsterdam . . . Cor! But we were hard boys, we knew that. We had the scars to prove it. We don't do too bad".

Patsy: "I mean there's Fred, he used to be an asphalter, and I used to be a totter, and here we are lunchin' wiv the stars. We worked hard for it . . . And fought hard.

"I mean, back to the Osmonds. Those little kids who follow them show no fear. We've nearly bin murdered lookin' after that band, and yet we never hit one of those little kids, and never would.

"When the Osmonds were stayin' at the Churchill there were a few guys goin' around posin' as security men. They were picking up little girls, and sayin' that if they er . . . went round the corner wiv 'em they'd see they got into the show free that night. These posers were molesting these little kids.

"When Fred and myself got wind of this, we found one of these guys, and he was molestin' this little kid. Well, he won't do it again . . ."

"You see", said Patsy. "we look after people".

Opposite:
Sly Stone
(*see page* 67)

Carly
Simon
(see page 102)

The Poets

Leonard Cohen

by Roy Hollingworth

"Let's sing a song boys. . . . This one has grown old and bitter' "—fragment from "Songs of Love and Hate", Leonard Cohen.

There was this room. Two storeys up from wet Holborn. It was a damp room, and on the floor of it—covered in paper and an old cardboard coffee cup—was a gold record.

It bore the legend "Songs of Leonard Cohen — 250,000 U.K. Sales". Gold discs look cheap when you look at them closely. But this one didn't.

"He's coming at 4 p.m.—er, I'll put you in a room," said somebody. "Do you drink? What do you want? Will scotch do? I think there's some in the other room," said the somebody. The room was depressing.

CBS in motion . . . crank, . . . ring . . . phone . . . bla . . . crank.

"He's in reception. . . . For God's sake get somebody down there! He's in reception, and he's talking to the receptionist. Get somebody down there, and get him up here. He's in reception. . . . Would you believe that. He's standing in reception!"

CBS people functioned. Somebody was sent down to get him—but he'd already come up—hands in pockets, smiling in a whimsical way. I think he was wearing carpet slippers. He looked smaller than he did the last time I saw him.

But it was unmistakably Cohen.

A day's growth lay black across his olive-skinned chin and cheeks. He stood, and looked somehow pointless. Stood, surrounded by people who were fussing. He wanted no fuss. He didn't talk to them, but meekly followed the mass of instructions he was being given, "Come this way, we'll do this now. . . . Can you come here? . . . I'm so-and-so Mr Cohen."

To all intents and purposes he looked like some half-tramp who'd been brought in from the cold, and was about to receive the sort of treatment old tramps are given every now and then. You know, they're given a meal, champagne, and put in the best hotel and they appear as chatty stories in the *Mirror* or the like.

Still smiling this strange, but warm smile he half-followed the "scene". Still with hands in pockets. Then a look spread over his face—I think I was the only one to catch it. It was a look of "What am I doing here? I don't want to be here." It vanished quickly.

They — CBS — fussed, and continued to fuss, and after five minutes the two of us had been ushered like children into this even smaller room.

It contained a large desk, behind which was a large dudey chair. In front of the desk was a narrow wooden chair, slightly lower than the other.

Cohen—now a little more relaxed, took the small chair, slumped, and sat in a huddle. It can only be described as a huddle, for he still refused to take his hands out of his pockets. I lounged into the big bosses' chair.

We exchanged pleasantries. It was nice to see each other again. It was.

"I feel like a boss man in this chair. Have you come for the job?"—I spoke.

"Actually, that's not such a jest," said Leonard, laughing a little. "I could do with a job." His hands came out of his pockets. One hand dropped a pack of Turkish cigarettes on the table—the other hand took a Turkish cigarette, and then both hands lit it, and delivered it to the mouth.

An unusual conversation followed.

It went a little something like this.

You've been in England for a while now. What have you been doing?

He began to croak. His voice was very croaky, and slow, and drawn out. His words were punctuated with sighs.

"Yeah, I've been here for a while off, and on. You see it's all been to do with this film they made of me on the European tour last year. It was a case of me wanting to cut out of everything indefinitely—but to leave a film of me for what you might call promotional purposes.

"So a film crew followed me around 23 cities, and spent an enormous amount of money. It was my money. I was paying for the film. Well, the film was shot, and when all the concerts were finished I was happy. I wanted to get out of the scene, and just forget it.

"But a couple of months later we get a call saying that the film's ready. So we fly to London, and see the film, and well, it's totally unacceptable—so like that was 125,000 dollars on something that was totally unacceptable. That's a lot of money, and I don't really have all that much money.

"Yet I was in a financial crisis, and something had to be done with it. I think there still might be a film of sorts. It was something I didn't want to go through—I just wanted the film done, and then get out of the scene."

You say, "get out of the scene". What do you mean?

"Well, I'm leaving. I'm leaving now."

Are there any specific reasons for you leaving?

"Oh well, I don't want to cut out completely. I want to continue writing songs, but I want to return to another rhythm; a rhythm I'm more used to."

You don't want any sort of "one album a year" thing then?

"Well (laughing a little), they never got me to do that anyway. I don't write *that* many songs. You know, my interests are in other places now. At one time I really thought music had some sort of social import—now it's just music . . . wonderful.

"You know I like to listen to music myself, but, well, I don't feel I want to have the same involvement with it. It's over."

He talked of the rhythm he wanted to find. . . . And that would be found in maybe a monastery.

"I want to think about things in a more direct way. You can't overlook the fact that you get to a stage with records when you're purely doing it for money—you know you try and keep something going. But you've got to pay attention to the thing. Sure you can leave it all to the hands of others—but when you see them put back an echo that's so distorted you realise that it's you who has to pay attention—all the time. If you don't want to pay attention—well, then you cut out.

"The public may not know whether I've cut out or not. I don't know how it will appear. There will be a record every now and then."

What do you feel about *these* people Leonard? I mean there's an album in a room back there which they're going to present to you. It's for 250,000 sales.

"Right. Oh if I have songs, then they'll be recorded. But first I have to make sure that I go away, and find a style of life I'm more suited to. Somehow I haven't organised my life within rock very well. Somehow IT—the rock life—became important; rather than the 'thing' that produced the song."

I feel *that* feeling is at a high in rock at the moment. There are a lot of people who have suddenly found that they've lost themselves. There's much disillusionment about. Do you agree?

"I don't even want to talk about it. I don't want it to be the substance of an interview. But look, write anything you want. I don't like hearing myself speak about the problem. To me, you know, it's the substance of an interview, like how they say in the monastery: 'May all beings accomplish whatever tasks they are engaged upon'.

"Well, I wish everybody well on 'the rock scene', and may their music be great. May there be some good songwriters—and there will. But I don't wanna be in it.

"I have songs in the air, but I don't know how to put them down. Anyway, I'm going."

Have you been writing much recently?

"I've found myself not writing at all. I don't know whether I want to write. It's reached that state. I have a book of poems out, and I'm pleased with them. But I don't find myself leading a life that has many good moments in it.

"So I've decided to screw it. And go. Maybe the other life won't have many good moments either . . . but I know *this* one, and I don't want it.

"No matter how withdrawn you feel from the scene—no matter how protected you think you are. No matter how little you think you're really involved with it. . . . You find yourself drawn into it.

"You find yourself worrying like 'I should have another song. I should write this. I should do better. I should appear more in public. I should be greater. I do envy that song, I do envy this one.' Well . . . forget it.

"I just feel like I want to shut-up. Just shut-up."

It wasn't an interview. We were just talking. The next topic was Derby County v Tottenham Hotspur. That may sound a bizarre thing to talk about.

We shared each other's feelings for the state of the music business. Goddamit, I nearly gave it all in right there and then—but thought "no", people have to read what this man is saying.

"Make this your last interview," said Leonard. "And let's both quit together." We'll see.

Dylan disappeared successfully—and came back. What do you feel about that?

"Yeah, he did, and I admire him. I've heard stories about him, and I've heard his music, but I don't know him personally. Yeah, he did get out of the public's eye. But you see I have a different problem—I've never been in the public's eye. But even so, I just wanna take off. I don't want to hear about this business. I want to get back to working."

Are you going to vanish forever—do you feel it's going to be a permanent thing?

"I've no idea. It's not like I'm announcing my retirement. No, not at all. It's a totally psychic thing, on a very private level. It may turn out that the public won't realise any difference. It may turn out that the records still keep coming, and the books keep coming. But I won't be there, I won't be part of it. Can you see what I mean?"

Yes.

"It's really ironic," he continued, "that there's that gold record out there, because it's come at the very end of things.

"I finished work yesterday, I'm going back to the States tomorrow. That's that. It's over. I'm off. I have nothing to do, no concerts, no commitments."

You've obviously made enough to exist off the money you have then.

"Well, this film's been a blow financially, but I don't have a great deal of bread. Well, I don't really know." He stopped and smiling, said "My lawyer tells me I have money. But I never see it."

I think I want to go away too—I said. But I know damned well I haven't got any money.

"But do it," he said. "This is the time. This is the time to retire to another life. This is a time to retreat.

It's a time when inferior men are coming forward, and the scene is being taken over by men who are rather shoddy. This is a purely personal feeling, from personal experiences.

"They may want to make me a bigger star—but I have other plans."

Is it totally ego?

"I think it's a matter of pride. Yes pride, and manliness, and dignity. It's a subtle thing. I mean we're not doing anything different than when we sat down and talked a year ago. But in the last 12 months we've been feeling things, a lot of us have been feeling things. A lot of us have seen what's been happening to this scene.

"I feel happy now. Happy that I've made my decision. Now I have no problems."

The room now seemed to be a sealed chamber—a sort of timeless zone. Cohen emits a charisma of tranquility, of calmness, and a very beautiful warmth. We smiled, and smoked cigarettes, and talked about New York City, and drugs, and other things.

I heard there were some weird things going on with the tour. Something went wrong in Tel Aviv didn't it?

"Yeah, there was a riot. We were supposed to be playing a small hall—2 to 3,000 people. Well, when we got off the 'plane they drove us into this sports arena! It was huge—there were about 10,000 people there. Well, that would have been okay. Horrible, but okay.

"Anyhow, nobody was allowed to be seated on the floor—so the audience was about a quarter of a mile away. They had huge speakers—about six feet tall."

"So I asked the people to come down, and sit closer to me, and they started to come, and the usher wouldn't let them. It wasn't a serious riot, but one or two people got it. It made me sad.

"Then there was Jerusalem, which was beautiful. It was sort of the end then. It was planned to be a sort of farewell tour. I was going around playing for the people I'd been writing for . . . and then it was all over."

He paused, and gently rubbed the side of his nose, gently stroked his chin, and then held both hands out—a gesture of an emotion about to flow.

"I feel it in my hands when I pick up the guitar. I feel that I'm no longer learning, and that my life is not right for it. I began to feel I was doing some of the songs a dis-service. So I have to get into something else."

His voice had now dropped to a low, croaking whisper. His lips hardly moved, but his eyes were fixed clearly and firmly on mine whenever he spoke. He lit another cigarette, and smoked it in a very soft way.

If you could—how-they say—'Do it all again' would you do it all again?

"What I wanted to do was to make one record, and have it reach a lot of people. I had a feeling that the songs I had written were destined for people, I didn't have a 'private' feeling about them. I knew my work was for people.

"But it didn't happen like that. It took a number of years to reach people, and somehow I got involved with the 'market place', and I got involved with my progress . . . which I never wanted. It didn't happen overnight, like I wanted it to. I thought it would.

"But, as I say. It took time. And now it's incredibly ironic that after five years there's this gold disc . . . (a half-laugh) five years!

"It's curious," he added.

Yes, it's curious.

"Yeah, I suppose I'd do it again, because I suppose I was doing what I wanted to do."

A completely private conversation followed—again regarding our disillusionment with rock, again regarding it being a time to leave.

"Maybe you should write that we both sat down, had a private conversation and both quit. Maybe you should do that. Just write that."

It's the stuff of story-books, really, how Cat Stevens contracted tuberculosis and fought the good fight against both tuberculosis and a lightweight pop image to emerge with a significant artistic identity.

There's even a touch of excruciating irony to this glossy cliché.

"I keep wondering what the inside of my lungs look like," he told the Melody Maker in 1967.

"But smoking calms me— although that's probably all psychological." A few months later he went into hospital.

There was probably a strong element of psychology, too, in the fact of his becoming ill.

He had been unhappy with his record company, Decca, who had insisted on his conforming to a "track record" based on "Matthew And Son" and hadn't—he alleged— given him the freedom to evolve.

He worried about what he considered the constricting pressure, and, as his body succumbed, his mind dried completely, like a lake. His period of convalescence he spent in refilling it.

These days, he worries, too, but the pressures are different. In the past three years since he signed with Island and made five albums, all models of sensitivity, he has gradually but with increasing momentum hove into view as a singer and songwriter of rare delicacy, a James Taylor with a breath of warm mystery. And while his sense of artistry has been expanding, so too has responsiveness among the public and the media.

He has reached that point of eminence where his performances are generally restricted to international tours.

The Sunday Times set the seal on his public approval in 1972 with a colour supplement spread, illustrated with pics by David Bailey, and as if to reinforce this air of voguishness his voice plays gently and romantically in the fashionable women's boutiques of Chelsea.

The image is correspondingly glamorous. He's a beautifully photogenic young man, with curly black hair and beard that emphasise his Greek background.

Since his manager, Barry Cross, also acts for several famous actors, including Peter Finch, one may infer this aspect has not exactly been underplayed.

He has a reputation too for high class chicks. He lost Patti D'Arbanville to Jagger, but celebrated it with a good song.

And there was also a liaison in 1971 with Carly Simon, which seems to have been dangerous but certainly inspired another two songs. She sang about him (among her other men) on one of her albums.

This desirable milieu is gratifying, but it makes him anxious. He finds it difficult to come to terms with his comparatively recent elevation. He thinks his songs are sometimes too shallow. He doesn't even rate himself very highly as a writer—or as anything, in fact.

Before he used to use other, more successful musicians as his artistic yardstick. Now he's one of the comparisons, and he feels uncomfortable.

This is misplaced modesty. In his best work he invests lyrics that seem to spring naturally from his sub-conscious with an exquisite sensibility, creating moods of eloquent sadness. He's sentimental, but in a genuinely romantic, uncloying, fashion.

"How Can I Tell You," for example, is a beautifully fragile ballad, a love letter whose lines are unformalised because the writer can only express a plea: "How can I tell you that I love you, but I can't think of right words to say."

His most telling songs are like

The Poets
Cat Stevens
by Michael Watts

this: they sound instantaneous, from the heart, as if it were unnecessary for each word to be weighed and evaluated in its context. They bear very much an emotional, and not intellectual, quality.

So many of his songs, accordingly, involve women, usually as they're leaving him. To these he can be patronising, even.

"It's hard to get by just upon a smile," he reminds the chick, in "Wild World". It's as if he can't resist a parting shot.

Often, when he's not remarking upon this relationship of his with women, he's trying to capture a dreamlike state, where subconscious images are allowed to link as they wish.

"Leaping and hopping on a moonshadow" . . . "Moonshadow" has the feel of a dream. He wrote it, he says, on arriving one night in Spain, when it was black and everything looked so unnatural.

"Into White," with its slow-motion rhythm, has the similar elusiveness of a state of trance, supported by a childlike wonderment in the lyrics. He writes of a house "built from barley rice, green pepper walls, and water ice," all "emptying into White".

There's a remarkable metaphysical resemblance with "Lucy In The Sky With Diamonds". It seems, in fact, to be the re-creation of an acid trip. He says he dropped a tab and the whole thing hit him suddenly—white!

"I'd been trying for 12 hours to get out of this door—it was open but I couldn't leave—and I finally got out and it was . . . snowing." "Lilywhite" evokes the same experience.

Cat Stevens, or Steve Georgiou, to give him his real name, was brought up as the youngest child of a Swedish mother, Ingrid, and a father Stavros, who comes from Thessalonika but has some Egyptian blood in him.

His father, says Cat, was always a lone Greek among the community here. "Belos" as they called him. Mad. The position of his restaurant, for example, the Moulin Rouge in Shaftesbury Avenue, instead of Camden Town or Charlotte Street, slightly separated him from the other Greeks.

"Father And Son" on "Tea For The Tillerman" would appear to describe the relationship between himself and his old man. It's a dialogue between the two characters, the father doling out paternal advice to quell the restiveness of his son: "you will still be here tomorrow but your dreams may not." On his side

the son complains bitterly that he has to break away, rejecting the advice to settle down and marry. "It's always been the same old story," he sings, "From the moment I could talk I was ordered to listen."

There's a strong traditional bond between Mediterranean families and it sounds as if young Steve was trying to sever it.

Looking back into his past, he says now, he realises he was influenced by his London environment to think it right and proper to pull as many chicks as he could—he makes ticking motions with his finger. But his elder sister, Anita, banned the idea of sex.

"She was very strict, so Victorian. She used to look after me when my mother was in the shop, and I'd be locked in cupboards for thinking things or getting hard about something." He smiles wanly.

"I've grown up with this terrible insecurity as to whether I'm right in thinking this, you know."

He thinks "Father And Son" does have a basis in truth—and maybe "Matthew And Son" refers to it, too though more obliquely—but it's a funny thing, at times he almost feels the father.

"Sometimes I know I am the old man. I hit a note and I can hear my father's voice."

Though he minimises it, there's a perceptible Greek influence in his music, notably in his 7/8 rhythms and the occasional use of native instruments like a bouzouki, that can be traced to the days of his youth when his father would take him to local weddings. Then there would be dancing all night and the sound of violins played Greek-style.

"The way they play the violin is ridiculous. There's no style, it's just the feel of the note."

It was from his mother's family, however, that he discovered his artistic temperament. He had a Swedish uncle, named Hugo, a polio victim who was an artist. Steve had gone to school there when he was about eight. From that moment he wanted to translate what he saw into pictures and music.

He emerged first through art, which led to "terribly gory, bloodthirsty pictures".

He was fascinated by blood. Apart from romance, death, he says, has been the motif that has constantly entered his songs, often in the sense of a relationship ending. He's a fatalist, which is a characteristic of the Greeks with their concept of "moira".

It's a gross over-simplification, however, to think of him as a romantic, doom-laden figure from a Greek tragedy.

There's an intensity about him, true, but it derives partly from the way he concentrates on explaining his meanings.

In person he substantiates the feeling of his songs: that he's intuitive, rather than a reasoning intellect.

After spending an afternoon with him I came away with the impression of an engaging but artless Cockney, who suggests none of the exoticness of his records.

His attraction for women is exotic enough, though. His songs about individual chicks are sort of dedications to each one, he says, "like little pages of my book". He smiles softly.

"Oh, I love women!"

He did a gig with Carly Simon at the Troubadour in Los Angeles.

"She's so clever!" he shakes his head. "A heavy lady. Don't ever think 'Wild World' was built for her, she was well beyond that. I love independent women, but I'm looking for two things in a woman: it's gotta be independence, and yet that closeness."

("I'm looking for a hard-headed woman, one who will take me for myself, and if I find my hard-headed woman I will need nobody else . . ." From "Tea For The Tillerman" album.)

He still sings all his songs about past affairs. "Lady D'Arbanville" he played to Patti—while she was in France—over the phone. She'd loved it. His songs were invariably about women as they walked away. And they were constantly walking away.

"Or I'm constantly falling asleep on them," he laughs. "I've never never felt satisfied, ever."

"Peace Train" he says—now that was a completely pornographic song, a phallic theme, with the train zipping through the countryside—"boom, boom, boom, y'know, till the climax at the end. I'd have to get a hell of a lotta women in to do that! I couldn't do that top note."

"Mona Bone Jakon" was similarly a phallic title. It was his little inword for a penis.

"I've come to the conclusion that anything other than being alone is false reassurance, even the idea of having a family, because all families disappear at death. So I don't like to get attached to anybody or anything."

To this end he lives alone in a

three-storey house in Fulham. He lives on the top floor in a white-painted loft. Downstairs in the basement there's an eight-track studio being built.

On the floor above is a relaxation pit with stereo equipment around the walls. There are very few records. He's given most of them away. He doesn't want to become too attached to possessions.

His songs, he explains, are empty statements which can be filled in by the person who's listening with his own colours. Each song was almost like a cloud; it might've moved by the time you looked for it again.

There's a song on his "Catch Bull At Four" album, which for once is a statement with a big S. Called "Ruins" it's a long epic, stark in words and music, about decay and destruction, containing an allusion to Vietnam.

"It's as close as I'll ever get to Vietnam—I won't even say the word. I had to imagine London, and in my mind I saw Oxford Street and the whole of my childhood, 'cause I'm trying to imagine when everything I know has been torn down."

This album, he says, was more polished, the images more crystallised.

"I had to make sure that the thought was inspired, and yet look back and psychoanalyse it whilst writing the lyrics. Still keeping in mind what I'm writing about, but looking on the other side at the same time."

It was crucial to his development, he explains, because he felt he was in danger of becoming a safe artist, a security to other people's heads.

He was getting terribly paranoid about Cat Stevens being a certain thing, a definite mood. Security was absolute death.

"Morning Has Broken," for instance, had been a chancey undertaking. He had just picked up a hymn book to get another perspective on lyrics, and he'd seen this one song.

It was the first one he decided to try to read (he can't read music). The main melody and the words (by Eleanor Farjeon) were already there, but he'd figured out the chords himself and Rick Wakeman had arranged the piano breaks.

It was the first song he'd ever sung on record that wasn't his, and he'd had no idea it was rooted in the tradition of school morning assemblies.

"I thought it was a hidden tune. That song, they said, I used to sing it! Some people said it was re-creation. I said it was recreation."

Eleanor Farjeon was dead, but he'd met one of the family and they'd been very happy about it. Now Nina Simone was cutting it.

"Teaser And The Firecat", on which "Morning Has Broken" was included, was really the springboard for his current success.

He writes and draws a 21-page child's book based on Teaser, and there's a similar cartoon story, using Spike Milligan's voice.

The story-line was disarmingly naive. "It has to do with the moon falling down from the sky and Teaser getting involved with the moon, which turns out to be a flat disc, and they get into weird adventures."

He explained the musical logistics of that album. The firecat had been the soul of the music, and the teaser had been the one who brought in the clever little lyrics here and there, or changed the time signatures.

"Catch Bull At Four" is less fanciful, more philosophic. The cover is focussed on a big circle, within which an Oriental is engaging the horns of a bull. The title was derived from Zen's ten stages of enlightenment.

He looked upon "Mona Bone Jakon" as being one, "Tea For The Tillerman" as two, and so on up to four.

"Catch Bull" was a very big step, he explained: "It's not something that I want to be taken lightly by myself. The eighth is a complete circle, I think, containing nothing.

"By the time I reach it I'll probably have stopped making records."

Miles Davis

by Michael Watts

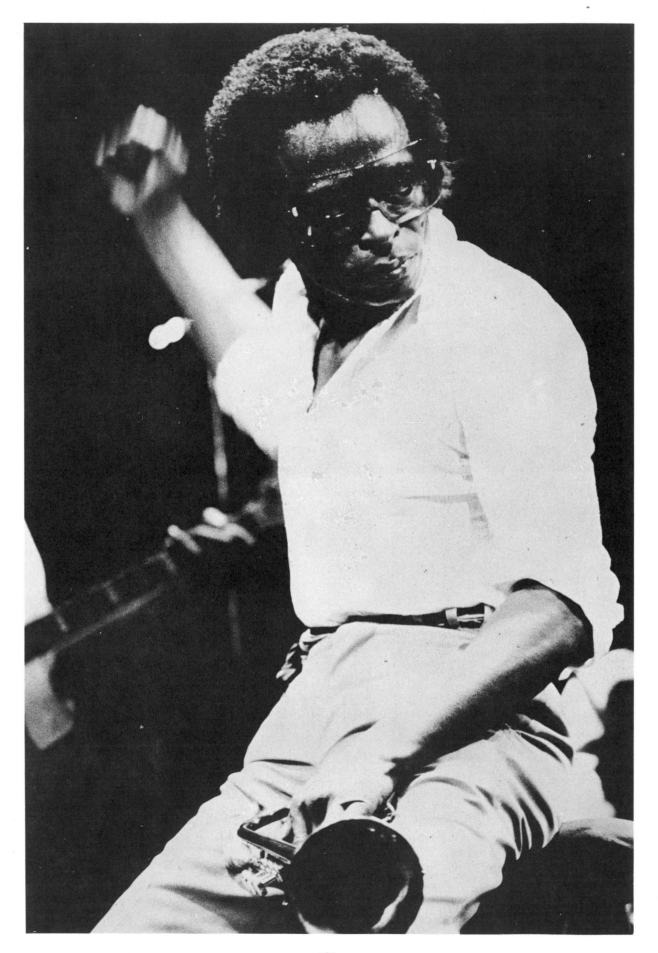

God, people keep moaning, all these rock and roll superstars, and how many of them know even how to act like a STAR, let alone a superstar!

It's so depressing for these taste-makers. You know, all they really want to do is swoon at someone's feet, someone with IT, the indefinable quality, and be rewarded with a few crumbs and maybe a benign pat on the head, just like it was in Holly-wood in the good old days. Hell, they don't even mind being kicked around a little, as long as they can get close to . . . a somebody. But now! Why, who acts more like a superstar, us or them?

Nobody ever had to explain this to Miles Davis. It's something he knew instinctively the moment he first put that horn to his lips. Man, he was a star and the whole god-damned effing world was gonna know it! And more than that, he was gonna rub their noses in all that fame of his, and do it with all the black arrogance he could muster.

So all those whiteys bought his records, told him they were *mad* about him, went to his concerts in droves—well, he was just gonna turn his back and play that trumpet, look cold and mean and splendid in the spotlight, and let them come to him, because he was Miles and didn't even need a surname to be remembered by. Just Miles.

And him playing jazz, too—jazz in this time of rock and roll, and theatre rock and soul! Especially soul, what with Sly Stone and all.

So here he is, a black man in his forties who plays trumpet of all things, not even guitar, and he's a bonafide superstar, the ONLY jazz superstar as far as all those out there in the great global village of rock and roll and beyond are concerned. Ask them. "Well, I don't really like jazz, but Miles Davis, sure, I've heard of him." It's really sweet.

Yes, it's sweet to have the man at Columbia Records ring up and say, "Hey, Miles, I have a cat here who wants to do an interview with you sometime this week," and for him to croak over the telephone in that weird voice of his: "Not this week, man; if he wants to do it he's gotta do it right now, right this hour, right this minute, right NOW! That's called being Miles, and the hell you don't do it his way!

So sure, I dropped everything. I got a cab straightaway and went out to his place on West 77th, and I didn't even have to look for the number to know Miles lived there.

Amid the sheer perpendicularity of those towering concrete blocks was this rococo house front inset with two arched, heavy wooden doors and looking like the El Morocco club someplace. I chose the door on the left, which opened easily, and stood in a small, stone entrance.

On my right were the speaker buttons for the four apartments in the building, but before I could press the one furthest left, marked "Davis", a door opposite swung open and there was this young guy who seemed to have been waiting for me all the time.

Although he was black his hair was thick and straight, like a white boy's, and combed right back. He wore a beard and a faintly amused expression, like "boy, do you know what you've let yourself in for?"

A flight of stairs was facing, but we entered a door on the right. Inside there hung a pale gloom, like that of a church vestry, which tapered away in the left direction to stark, cold light, splashing through cream-stucco arches and disclosing a small, walled courtyard at the end. But here in the darkness, lit by a softly-glowing light, was the centre-piece: an electric organ, with a large, beaten gong hanging just beyond the keyboard, like an instrument of Damocles.

There was a tiger's head resting with bared teeth in one corner and a stack of black amplifiers in the other. On top of them lay a pale green horn and a sign made out of thick cardboard, like those that hotel guests can hang outside their doors. It said: No Visitors.

The guy, thickset and in jeans, led the way up a short flight of steep stairs set against a wall opposite. At the top it was even darker, with a clinging, musky smell. As I came off the top step, blinking, I was con-fronted with a small open alcove made in what appeared to be dark marble. One side was a large mirror; the nearest side was scooped out. Through it I could make out the upper half of a reclining figure, red-shirted back propped against a chair, legs clothed in beige, tartan slacks resting on a marble shelf. It was un-clear at first, even though the alcove was brightly lit, because of the surrounding darkness.

I walked around the alcove, through another arch, and was suddenly brought up to find myself in a bedroom. The bed lay in a pit and in the bed, tangled in the white sheets, was a light-skinned girl lying fast asleep. I paused and looked back into the alcove. The figure was regarding me with sombre eyes. The hair was wet and its damp straggles were now being combed by the first guy.

The face was very dark and its bones were fine, even delicate, but under the bright bulb it seemed shrunken and pinched. The eyes were huge, like a bushbaby's orbs, almost impoverishing the rest of his features, and they just stared and stared. It was a full 30 seconds before I realised I was looking at Miles Davis. "Huh?" he croaked, so low I could barely hear him.

Miles' voice is a phenomenon. It's a hoarse whisper, strained through his larynx like a sieve. He dredges it up slowly through the whole of his body, but it barely leaves his lips. It just hangs, a vague sibilance in the air, like the effort of a dying man. At first it's both incomprehensible and comic. Instinctively you cock your head to one side to catch what he's saying. But gradually, you adjust to its level, as you would twiddle the dials on a radio to get its tuning.

"Hi," I blurted. He just kept on staring slowly around him, as if it was painful to speak. I shifted awkwardly. There were bottles and lotions on the shelf. The air was heavy with the smell of something. It was quiet, a thick, carpeted silence, except for the gentle swish of the comb and the occasional click of the scissors wielded by his barber-cum-personal assistant.

Nothing was said. Until: "How long was you waiting to press that bell?" he enquired at last in that peculiar whisper. "Ten maybe 15 seconds," I replied in a somewhat hushed voice. In that atmosphere a hush seemed appropriate. "We was having a bet," he explained slowly. "Yeah, see, you owe me five bucks," said his assistant quite loudly. To me: "We were betting how long it'd take you to ring."

Miles waved his hand loosely. "Take a look around downstairs, if you want to," he said, but I didn't hear him at first. "What?" He repeated it. I went down to the first floor.

Past the vestry there was a fur rug on the slabbed floor. It opened out into an airy room with a couch, and beyond more arches was a wide, glass window from floor to ceiling. Against one wall was a chromium-gleaming porterised bed. A reminder of his accident of two months ago when he crashed his Lamborghini and broke both ankles. I climbed the stairs again.

He was still there, though for some reason I hadn't expected him to be. The silence was pregnant with possibilities. But after a few minutes he eased himself out of his chair and came slowly towards me. I realised suddenly that although apparently recovered his legs still pained him.

He pushed me over to the dark section of the room, which was elevated from the rest, found a Sony cassette machine and inserted a small tape. He motioned to the floor. "Siddown, siddown," he breathed heavily, and then leaned over and literally jammed these headphones over my ears. "My new album," he muttered, and pressed the button.

What I heard was obviously unfinished but undeniably exciting. Fiercely percussive—there were three drummers—it consisted of a circular rhythm, almost a loop, that was the nearest thing to a soul groove that I've yet heard from him. Horns were kicking along with the rhythm and he was playing electric piano. It sounded like the next step on from his "On The Corner" album, which in turn has an affinity with Sly Stone's music.

Miles disappeared into the bedroom and I looked around me. In the half-light rested a large, semicircular sofa made of some hide, in front of which was a table that held a wire sculpture which bobbed and weaved when you touched it. Miles the boxer, I thought obliquely. Packed tight behind this was a piano, jammed almost up against a shelf containing four track cartridges.

On a low table rested a gold-plated Bell telephone, one of those early-style instruments which have become voguish in the past two years, and on top of the piano a gold record for "Bitches Brew". More golds lined the walls. An unopened bottle of Valpolicella stood forgotten on a shelf. And over all this was that indefinable musk.

The master returned, only to beckon me into the bedroom. I was beginning to think he was house proud, in his way. Also, I was starting to wonder when he'd loosen up enough to talk. "I ain't been to sleep for three days," he croaked at me, as if by way of explanation. "Been making this music." Then: "Go on, have a look in there." He was pointing to the bathroom. I did as I was told.

In the bedroom he was looking through a long rack of clothes. The chick still lay coiled in the same position. Two colour televisions flickered noiselessly on each side of the bed. The house appeared without much life or cheer. But there was the animation of his presence, dark and unsmiling.

"Be right with you," his face flashed at me. I went back and sat on the sofa to wait. I calculated that in the past half-hour since I'd entered the place he'd said maybe half a dozen sentences. I pushed the wire sculpture and half-consciously sparred with it, then glanced at a car brochure for a Duster Valiant Barracuda. It was a well-founded reputation, I thought.

He was around fifteen more minutes. In that time two white musicians arrived and one began to play the electric organ downstairs, the other had a sax. Also in the meantime his assistant went into the bedroom with his scissors and what seemed to be a stretch bandage. At one time I heard a hoarse scream followed by "I———" that was clearly audible. And then he came out. He'd put on shoes, his red shirt was buttoned up, and his hair, receding a little at the sides, was all prettified. It was as if he had to face the world on his terms.

He sat right up close to me and rasped, in a voice like a thin file, "Whadda ya wanna know? whadda ya wanna know?" The organ was playing distantly, ethereally. Very unreal.

I asked him who was playing on his new album. Well, it seemed like as good an opening as any.

"I'm not gonna tell you," he whispered from about nine inches away. "Nobody's ever heard of 'em. New guys. One's a statistician; he's an Indian. I don't wanna tell their names, y'know, because critics . . ."

"Miles!" The chick's voice came from within the bedroom, and then she appeared in the entrance, wrapped in a towel or something.

"Yes, babe," he said. She looked at the two of us and disappeared. He looked at me, frowning at the question he'd forgotten.

The critics?

He settled slowly into an answer. "Yeah, I don't put any names or instrumentation on it, and then the critics 'll have to listen. I'm not gonna tell you what's on it, man. Whatever you think is on it. You know, I get tired of people . . . critics. They don't do anything in this business. Without a musician's record what's a disc-jockey—nothing.

But. . . .

"There's no but, there's no but," he rapped sharply. "There's no critic in the world that knows as much as I do. There's no but, period."

Did that go for black and white critics? He stared hard. "It goes for critics even if they're green! Sheeit! All black musicians don't have rhythm, y'know." He looked back at his hands. "But I didn't put those names on 'On The Corner' specially for that reason, so now the critics have to say, 'what's that instrument, and what's this?' I told them not to put any instrumentation on but they did. I'm not even gonna put my picture on albums anymore. Pictures are dead, man. You close your eyes and you're there."

I asked what he was going to put on future covers, then. He nodded to a stack of portfolios in a corner which were full of cartoons. "Things like that, man." He gave me a weary look. "You see, if I explain things they'll use it in London. My advice is expensive. You may have to watch that. People pick your brains. Every time Quincy Jones comes to town he comes here—and I dunno why! He just sits up here. If you don't have it in you there's nothing . . . you know." The notion of the critics struck him again. "They'll see your name," he said simply, "and say, 'oh, I know how he plays.' "

He picked up an acoustic guitar and ran his right hand aimlessly over the strings. "If you're a musician," he muttered, "you should always keep something in your hand." He plucked softly, and then gave the strings a savage slash. "Oh shit".

I mentioned that particular guitar. "Oh, Gil gave it to me when we made 'Sketches Of Spain', " he replied, then broke off, "I gotta have one of your cigarettes." He picked up the cigarettes and started undoing the already-opened pack from the wrong end. I had to help him.

"I've been up for three days," he explained again "writing this f——— music!" His accent was vituperative. "And Columbia ain't gonna sell it, anyway. They sell all the pretty, little faggot-looking white boys, that's their thing. I just got an offer from Motown for this new album.

"You know, I will make 500,000 dollars in a year, but I will do it for five dollars if my music would get to the black people, and Columbia couldn't get albums into Harlem." He played a loud discord. "That's what I'm told by the vice-president. He don't talk to me on the phone for nothing."

(After this interview I spoke to Bob Altschuler, director of infor-

mation services for Columbia, who pointed out amiably, as if he'd heard it all before, that there was no way Miles could leave the record company. He was under contract. "This is his way of pressuring Columbia," he said. "We talk to him every day. He needs reassurance.")

Miles was talking to his assistant, who was leaving, about some clothes. In a few days' time he was about to play two nights at the Village East, the old Fillmore. "They should have a Stirling Cooper over here," he muttered, and got up and walked to the bedroom to speak to the girl.

When he came back the white sax player was sitting down. He was bald on top with long hair down the sides and back, and wearing a pair of horn rims. "This is Dave Lieberman," Miles croaked. "He's on the album." The guy nodded silently. He sat listening without saying a word.

I reminded Miles he'd been accusing Columbia of not pushing his records in Harlem. "I'm not white and Jewish, man," he replied. But did he think more whites than blacks bought his records?

"I don't care who buys the records as long as they get to the black people, so I will be remembered when I die." He said the last sentence softly. "I'm not playing for any white people, man. I wanna hear a black guy say, 'yeah, I dig Miles Davis. I'd like to play like that.' I'm not prejudiced, you know. But I lean towards that. It would knock me out if a little kid . . . y'know, the closest thing that happened to me was that the doctor brought his son over to the hotel and his son was asking him why don't he have a house like mine." He laughed for the first time.

"Aw, shit . . . But you know they sell a guy's ass down. Engelbert Humperdinck" — the name came haltingly off his tongue—"I never had any o' this. You know, whatchamacallit came by here, what's his name? A Rolling Stone."

Mick Jagger?

"Yeah, so Al (Aronowitz, the writer) said: 'Lemme in, it's Mick Jagger.' I said: 'Man, sheeit! F— Mick Jagger.' I was f———, man. why should I let him in? Maybe if it had been Ray Robinson." He paused and threaded his fingers across the guitar strings.

I mentioned to him that Jagger had gone to see Chick Corea, his former alumnus, down in the village, and that Chick had done pretty well when he played Ronnie Scott's in London a couple of months back.

He turned and looked at me. "He did pretty well? You mean England did good." There was no answer to that.

I asked him when was the last time he'd played any clubs. He stopped plucking and tried to think. "I don't know. I can't remember." Then: "Denver, in October. Then, when I came home, I was driving and broke both of my ankles. I was cruising, y'know, but I was still up from that gig in Denver. I musta hypnotised myself 'cos I went right up fast."

A wet road? "Yeah. I was only doing about 30 miles an hour. I ran up on an island. I was just tired." Pluck, pluck. "I f——— the car up, but it wasn't a mess. I got a new un. A Ferrari." I'd already noticed a toy Ferrari lying on the table in front of us. Cars and horns — his two passions. And women.

"Y'know," he said after a while, "I'd rather play trumpet than f——— because you really get a thrill when you do somethin' with a group. I mean, it's something.' Anybody can f———. I think making love is a little bit, well . . ." He dissolved into deep, gruff mirth, like a wheeze.

I said, talking about trumpets, he didn't seem to be playing quite as much these days. There was less emphasis on notes and phrases.

"That's a matter of opinion," he answered abruptly. "When I was with Bird, Fats Navarro used to say I played too fast all the time, but I couldn't swing with Max Roach 'cos he couldn't swing. I mean, because you have technique you don't have to use it. You use it when you feel like it. I mean, you can run, but if you can walk you walk, right? You do what you gotta do. It's called good taste. I play whatever comes into my black head, man."

The critics, of whom he had been so contemptuous, had also claimed he'd been influenced the past couple of years by Sly Stone. I left the insinuation hanging in the conversation.

He drew his breath in. I wondered what he was going to say. "You ever hear Sly Stone play like 'On The Corner'?" he replied at last. It was one of those questions that wouldn't brook an answer.

A certain rhythmic . . . I began to say.

"We're both black!" he snorted. "I tell you something, man, it makes me so f——— mad when people say: 'This is influenced by this, this is influenced by that.' " He pointed to Lieberman, silent and intent in the corner. "*He* doesn't play like Coltrane, but the critics will say so! How the f——— am I gonna play like Sly Stone? Sly wants me to produce him! They have a nice group but . . . they don't have any intelligence man!" The last part of his sentence rose in a crescendo, as if any collaboration was somehow unthinkable.

But he listened? "Sure I listen to everybody." He stopped. "I don't listen to those white groups." He fumbled for another cigarette in my pack. The remnants of three others he'd lit lay in an ash-tray. Hardly smoked, they were three short columns of grey ash, smouldering. He rested the fourth cigarette in the tray and the fragile columns crumbled.

But, I persisted, how about Carlos Santana, say?

"Why should I play with him? No, I'd only be in his way. I just tell you this. They don't have the musical knowledge that Dave has." He pointed again. "Or me. Or Chick Corea. And neither did Jimi Hendrix. Jimi Hendrix could swing, but not with Mitch, with Buddy Miles. Boy, that album was outasight! Buddy gets so he sounds like a hillbilly, man." He chuckled "I mean, there's places to go. Jimi—he couldn't change. He hadda be brought up, he had to study. I started when I was 12."

A lack of musical education? Was that it?

"That's what it is, yeah. But you don't have to read. It's not necessary."

I asked how he found his musicians.

"I pick 'em up just like you pick up a girl." Laughter. "I don't go anywhere much, y'know. A lot of 'em come to me but I don't hire 'em. There's a lotta reasons. A guy might have too much ego and can't play with a group and be a good player."

But he seemed to have had a good working relationship with John McLaughlin?

"Yeah, he played different when he played with us. He gets it on. I got John set up, ain't that a bitch?" He was looking across at Lieberman, who just smiled faintly and said nothing. It amused Miles. "I got him set up! I sent him to Nat Weiss See, I know these people. When I make a record and it sounds good they say, 'well, that's Miles.' Y'know, it's supposed to sound good. That's why I'm leaving Columbia, man I'm not gonna give 'em this latest album.

I'm gonna give it nobody." There was a slightly gleeful look in his face.

But he'd release it sometime, surely?

"I'll erase it," he replied bluntly. "I told Clive (Davis, then head of CBS). Sent a telegram, told him he should get a black . . . he should use his sources all over the country and get a black man who thinks black to sell the music to black people, 'cos the white people seem to know about it. But everybody is scared to go into the black neighbourhood. Nobody gets up town, you know. And a lot of white musicians, they have friends up town. Shit . . . your record'll never get up there.

"See, I'm on the Columbia mailing list. I get a list and it's all white guys with long hair"—he ran his hands down the side of his face—"and pretty faces, trying to show their muscles and their pricks and stuff. I mean, what the f——— is that? I'm afraid to play the album, you know what I mean? I mean, it's great for white boys to say I'd like to look like that when I grow up, but what's the black boy gonna say?"

He leaned back against the sofa, as if he'd made up his mind on something. "No, no, I'm not getting into a discussion of white and black. I'm just saying that a Chinaman knows how to sell it, knows where it should go, but not me." He passed a hand wearily across his high forehead.

Did he feel exploited, then?

"I been exploited for ten years, man." But he could still make 500,000 dollars at the end of every 12 months.

"I don't even need it, man." He sounded very tired. "If I sweep your porch I'd get 15 dollars, but if I play trumpet on your porch it's a different thing." Silence.

Did this help to explain why when he was playing concerts, which usually have more whites than blacks, he turned his back on the audience?

"No, no, it has nothing to do with it." He stared very hard. Remember, his face was only a few inches from mine.

"What do you mean by turning my back on the audience?" His tone was very tart. "What should I do? Smile at 'em," he asked witheringly.

"I just do what I feel like doing. I have the product. I can dance and all that sh!t, and box, but I do it when I feel like it. Listen, man, listen"—impatient—"when I step out on that stage I don't even see those people, I don't care where it is. I can't be looking at those people and

thinking about what they think of me. I don't give a f——— what they think of me, here or any place else."

But it all contributed to his image. "There is no image, man." He said the word as if he'd never heard of it before. "If I don't concentrate on what I'm doing and listen I can't play the shit, and then they won't get anything. I mean, I can't be looking at some bitch, man, smiling and goin' on, even in my mind. If I did I'd take my horn down and go out and do that. Takes a lotta energy to play an instrument. I lose about four pounds." He laid the guitar aside and took out another of my cigarettes.

I decided to ask him again about his album. A young black guy, a dancer I later found out, was now in the room, listening to the Sony on the phones and now and then giving out a whoop.

I mentioned to Miles his electric piano playing. He was hunched over the guitar again.

"Well, I only play to get the idea how it's supposed to go," he said slowly, "but it always turns out that my piano playing—I hate that word 'better' but . . . it brings out the band, and doesn't clutter up too much, either. When I play piano in my band they swing. When my piano player plays they swing sometimes, but they don't swing all the time. I don't worry about anything 'cos I have reggie (I think he meant reggae, surprisingly enough), y'know, the rhythm swings, but you have to watch a musician and anticipate it."

I could hear the percussion sound on the tape, a hard, chunky pulse. Out of the blue I asked him if he'd ever heard of the Japanese percussionist, Stomu Yamash'ta. I told him he used about 40 percussion instruments on stage.

He gave me that intimidating stare of his. "What you askin' me for? He should be in a circus." The idea amused him. "Let him play on Christmas, and maybe Jesus'll come down."

Well, I had to laugh at that. Black humour is really, but really, the description for Miles.

I didn't get to hear anymore of it. He'd decided the interview was finished. He had to go downstairs and rehearse with Lieberman. He went into the bedroom and came out with a brown poncho. Very slowly he pulled it over his head and buckled a belt around his middle. The dancer asked incredulously if he was going out. Miles said nothing. Just walked painfully down those stairs. Never

said goodbye.

I put on my coat and talked to the dancer for a few minutes, took a last look around the dream home, and descended those stairs.

Miles hadn't left. He was standing against one of those Moroccan arches, a phone in his hand—one of those phones where the dial is set into the receiver. The fingers of his other hand were revolving the dial. He didn't look up as I spoke to him.

"Goodbye, it was good meeting you," I said.

He continued dialling. "Why?" he replied shortly.

I mumbled something, and held out my hand. He grasped it in his. "I don't mean to be rude," he said tiredly, "it's just . . . I haven't slept for three days."

He still hadn't taken his eyes off the phone.